21st Century Sustainable Homes

The publishers, Alessina Brooks and Paul Latham,
would like to dedicate this book to the memory of
architect and author **Dennis Sharp**, a long-time friend
of The Images Publishing Group and an early champion
of sustainable design.
His passion and enthusiasm will be greatly missed.

21st Century Sustainable Homes

Edited by Mark Cleary

images
Publishing

Published in Australia in 2011 by
The Images Publishing Group Pty Ltd
ABN 89 059 734 431
6 Bastow Place, Mulgrave, Victoria 3170, Australia
Tel: +61 3 9561 5544 Fax: +61 3 9561 4860
books@imagespublishing.com
www.imagespublishing.com

Copyright © The Images Publishing Group Pty Ltd 2011
The Images Publishing Group Reference Number: 942

National Library of Australia Cataloguing-in-Publication entry:

Author: Cleary, Mark W., 1971-
Title: Sustainable homes / Mark Cleary.
ISBN: 9781864704280 (hbk.)
Subjects: Sustainable architecture.
Sustainable design.
Architecture.
Dewey Number: 728.370472

Coordinating editor: Mark Cleary

Designed by The Graphic Image Studio Pty Ltd, Mulgrave, Australia
www.tgis.com.au

Pre-publishing services by United Graphic Pte Ltd, Singapore
Printed on 140 gsm Gold East paper by Everbest Printing Co. Ltd., in Hong Kong/China

IMAGES has included on its website a page for special notices in relation to this and our other publications.
Please visit www.imagespublishing.com

Contents

Introduction

We all know what sustainable means … kind of … vaguely. It means good for the environment. It means 'green', 'environmentally-friendly', 'eco-responsible'. Yes, 'sustainable' has joined the legion of ubiquitous catchwords used so often and in so many contexts any definitive meaning has been lost. This devaluation of the word has not been helped by its misuse and overuse in the world of marketing and advertising to sell products whose environmental benefits are sometimes questionable at best.

What, therefore, is a sustainable house? Must it be constructed entirely of bamboo, covered in solar panels, surrounded by water tanks and have a wind turbine in the front yard? Can a large house be considered sustainable? Is concrete a sustainable material? If so, are some forms of concrete more sustainable than others? How do we quantify or judge sustainability? By LEED accreditation? HERS points? Energy Star ratings? Adherence to the Code for Sustainable Homes? Do we factor in embodied energy levels or restrict ourselves to operating efficiencies in our definition of sustainability? And on and on the questions go.

21st Century Sustainable Homes does not propose to define precisely what makes a house sustainable. It does not put forward any single, definitive version of a sustainable house. Design, materials and construction methods have not been rigorously assessed to ensure they meet some pre-determined sustainability criteria. It may be that not all of the houses contained in this book can be considered 'sustainable' according to some very strict definitions of the word. Some are undeniably more 'sustainable' than others. Some were conceived with the idea of sustainability at their very core, while others just happen to have elements of sustainability because they make use of materials and natural climatic advantages recognised as being sustainable long before any threat of a warming planet.

What these houses point toward, to varying degrees, is our inevitable future. We must reduce our reliance on fossil fuels, we must make better use of renewable energies, we must reduce waste, and we must reuse and recycle more materials. But far from being a daunting prospect, the houses in this book show that sustainability can be achieved without any compromise in lifestyle, comfort or aesthetics; and it can often be achieved more simply, cheaply and stylishly than we might have imagined.

21st Century **Sustainable** Homes

100K House

Philadelphia, Pennsylvania, USA

Interface Studio Architects

Photography: Sam Oberter, Postgreen

The 100K House recognises the waste inherent in unnecessarily large houses.

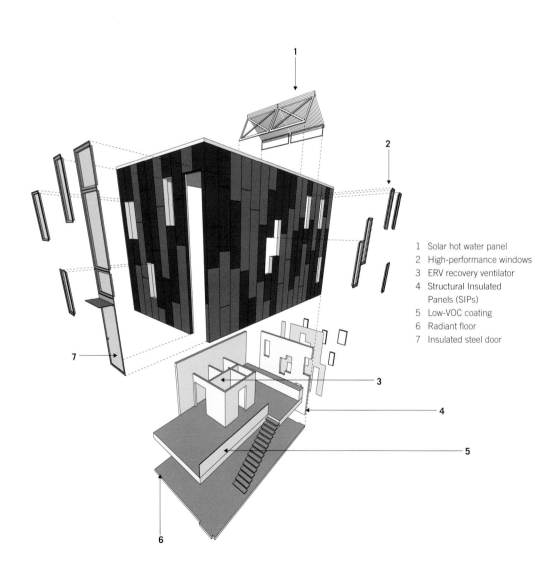

1 Solar hot water panel
2 High-performance windows
3 ERV recovery ventilator
4 Structural Insulated
   Panels (SIPs)
5 Low-VOC coating
6 Radiant floor
7 Insulated steel door

Before the Global Financial Crisis burst the bubble, the combination of low interest rates, conspicuous consumption and irrational confidence saw house sizes reach record levels, particularly in Australia and the US, where the average house size increased from 91 square metres (980 square feet) in 1950 to 218 square metres (2347 square feet) in 2004—a more than 140 per cent increase[1].

But the end of the housing boom has already started to rein things in, with the size of the average new US house shrinking by 7.52 square metres (81 square feet) in 2009 compared to the year before, as homebuyers start to appreciate the economic, if not environmental, benefits of a smaller home[2]. The logic is simple—a larger house requires more materials to build and more energy to heat and cool, typically increasing carbon emission levels expended in constructing and running it.

1 National Association of Home Builders (*Housing Facts, Figures and Trends for March 2006*)

2 US Census Bureau

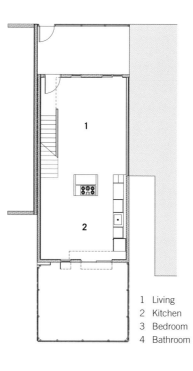

1 Living
2 Kitchen
3 Bedroom
4 Bathroom

0   2m

Ground floor

First floor

The 100K House recognises the waste inherent in such unnecessarily large houses. At 93 square metres (1000 square feet), it is less than half the size of the average US home, and uses cost-effective construction principles and simple, locally-sourced materials to ensure affordability for environmentally aware first homebuyers.

A passive strategy—focused on the building envelope more than systems—was employed in the 100K House design, which includes high levels of insulation and air sealing in combination with an energy recovery ventilator (ERV), producing energy efficiencies. The radiant floor slab, ductless air-conditioning unit and openings in the floor between levels create a convection circulation flow through the house, requiring minimal systems and no ductwork.

The idea of sustainability was implicit at every stage of 100K House's design, from its small size, framing module, insulation and sealing of the envelope, and local sourcing of components and materials. Every component, material, window, and flashing detail was conceived in terms of energy efficiency, culminating in the house's LEED for Homes Platinum certification and low HERS score, proving less really is more in terms of sustainability.

Aptos Family Retreat

Aptos, California, USA

CCS Architecture

Photography: Paul Dyer

Reclaimed barn wood for the exterior gives the house a rustic charm while minimising the use of new construction materials.

Leaving a shallow carbon footprint was an important concern for the owners of this country retreat on a 20-acre property in the Santa Cruz Mountains, inland from the beach town of Aptos in Northern California. The key architectural inspiration was the imagery of American barns, and through the use of reclaimed barn wood for the exterior the house is given a rustic charm while minimising the use of new construction materials.

A south-facing operable glass wall runs almost the entire length of the house's 'living' volume, letting in cooling summer breezes that circulate through the house. The overhang provides shade in summer while capturing the heat from the lower winter sun. Ventilation shafts incorporated in the design further assist passive cooling through the heat stack effect.

The high-performance glass provides effective insulation, keeping the heat in during winter and out during summer. The insulation is so effective that the radiant heating system in the lower and upper level floors is the house's only form of heating, apart from the fireplace.

Hot water for domestic use, for the radiant floor heating and for the pool is provided by an evacuated tube solar collector, a form of thermal solar heating that heats the water through a series of tubes located in the yard.

Cor-ten rusted steel, a high-content recycled product, was used for the roof of the main house, and for the walls and roof of the barn. Though steel may have high embodied energy levels, it is highly recyclable and long lasting, not requiring regular replacement like some other building materials. Metal roofs with heat deflecting coatings and finishes can also substantially reduce the amount of energy required for cooling.

With its charming rustic exterior and sensitivity to the environment, this open, light and casual mountain getaway complements rather than imposes upon its beautiful forest surroundings.

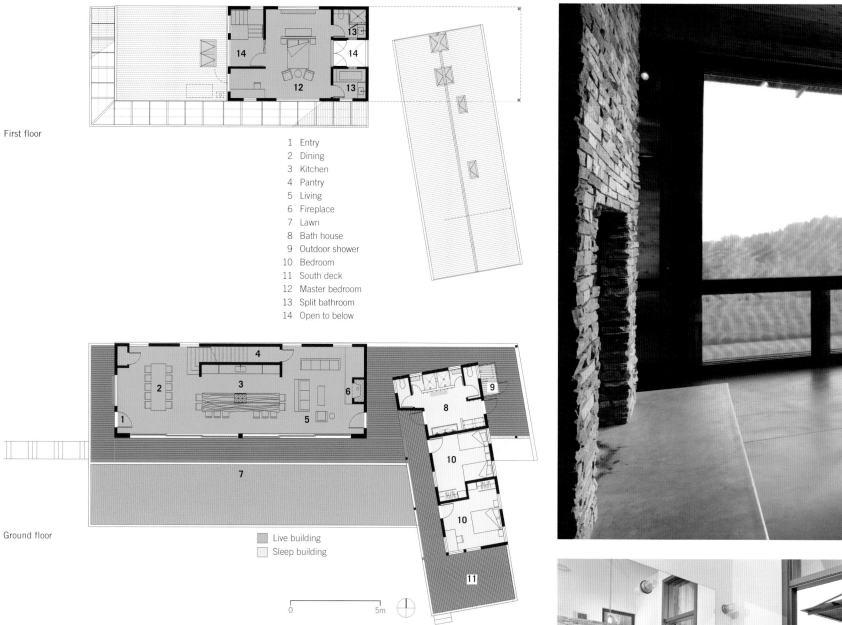

First floor

1 Entry
2 Dining
3 Kitchen
4 Pantry
5 Living
6 Fireplace
7 Lawn
8 Bath house
9 Outdoor shower
10 Bedroom
11 South deck
12 Master bedroom
13 Split bathroom
14 Open to below

Ground floor

Live building
Sleep building

0   5m

Arrowtown House

Arrowtown, New Zealand

Kerr Ritchie Architects

Photography: Paul McCredie

A combination of simple passive design elements and more sophisticated technology work in tandem to achieve energy efficiencies.

Local building regulations required the design of this house—located in the scenic former goldmining town of Arrowtown on New Zealand's South Island—to remain in keeping with the surrounding architecture. In part, this meant keeping it small, which is what the owners had in mind anyway, interested as they were in building a house with a minimal environmental impact.

In fact, the design intentionally makes the house appear more compact than it actually is by resembling a series of sheds. The environmental benefits of this relative small size (135 square metres, or 1453 square feet) are a lower level of embodied energy than an average-sized house (which in New Zealand is approximately 195

square metres, or 2100 square feet[1]), and the reduced energy consumption for heating and cooling a smaller space. Additionally, a lower plot ratio leaves more space on the site for the fruit and vegetable garden. The house is also located within easy walking distance of the town and to the workplace of one of the owners, reducing the need for car travel.

But it is not its compact size alone that qualifies the house as environmentally friendly. A combination of simple passive design elements and more sophisticated technology work in tandem to achieve energy efficiencies. With an average maximum winter temperature of 10 ˚C, and a minimum of just 1 ˚C, maintaining internal warmth is important.

The house is positioned to capture the heat from the winter sun, with the floor-to-ceiling windows double glazed and thermally broken, a superior form of insulation in which there is a space between both the glass and the aluminium joinery, retaining more heat than standard double glazing. Extra thick timber walls provide further insulation, and polished concrete floors thermal mass. A ground source energy system, which captures the earth's natural heat via a 120-metre (394-foot) vertical bore in the ground, provides energy-efficient heating when required.

The combination of sustainable design elements in Arrowtown House saw the architects awarded the 2010 BMW EfficientDynamics Sustainability award.

1   www.infometrics.co.nz

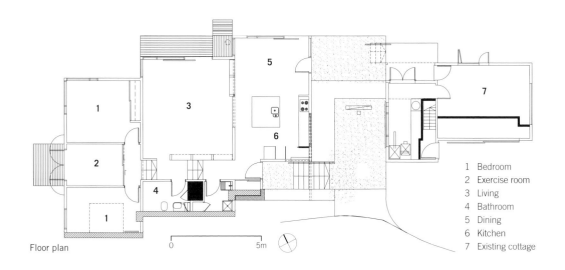

Floor plan

1 Bedroom
2 Exercise room
3 Living
4 Bathroom
5 Dining
6 Kitchen
7 Existing cottage

Autonomous House

Jan Juc, Victoria, Australia

Zen Architects

Photography: Sharyn Cairns

Thick mud render applied to the straw-bale walls helps maintain stable internal temperatures.

The Jan Juc Autonomous House is sited on a clearing made vacant by a fallen gum tree in bushland near Bells Beach. The naturally occurring clearing was chosen to minimise environmental disturbance and because the space provided excellent access to sunlight in an otherwise dense tree canopy.

The wishes of the owner and the remote nature of the site called for an autonomous building that harvested its own power and water and treated its own waste on site. The result is a house that utilises passive solar design for most of its heating and prevailing breezes for passive cooling.

The form of the house minimises its footprint by 'weaving' through the trees. The main entry hallway follows the path of a well-worn wallaby track that cascades down toward a seasonal creek. The darkness of the entry provides a dramatic contrast to the bright north-facing habitable rooms, giving the sensation of walking into a sunny clearing.

Recycled wharf posts are used as structural framing, continuing the rhythm of tree trunks in the dense forest outside the house. Radially sawn weatherboards are cut to minimise waste and detailed to resist bushfire attack.

Thermal mass in the form of an exposed concrete floor slab and the thick mud render applied to the straw-bale walls helps maintain stable internal temperatures and gives the house a feeling of thermal and acoustic solidity.

A stand-alone 3.3-kilowatt solar photovoltaic array and battery store provides all electricity and is backed up with a biodiesel generator. Integrated solar hot water and hydronic heating is boosted by a wood-fired stove boiler. All water is harvested and retained on site in 25,000-litre water tanks. All black and greywater is processed through a worm farm which irrigates the fruit trees and vegetables.

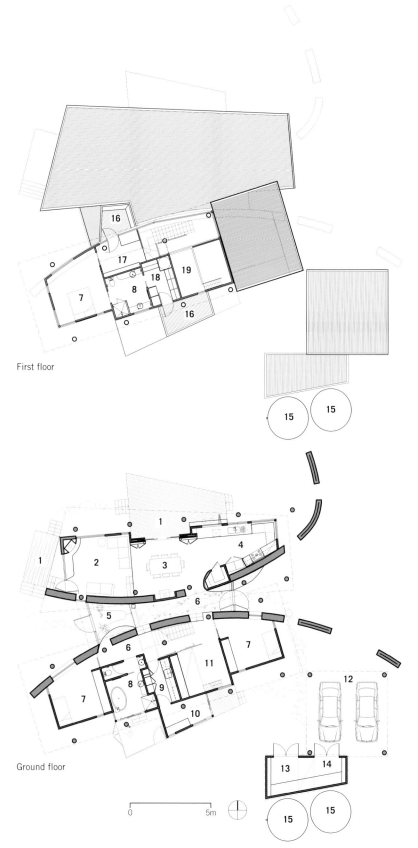

First floor

Ground floor

0   5m

1 Deck	11 Rumpus room
2 Living	12 Carport
3 Dining	13 Shed
4 Kitchen	14 Battery storage
5 Sitting room	15 Water tank
6 Hall	16 Balcony
7 Bedroom	17 Library
8 Bathroom	18 Walk-in-robe
9 Dry room	19 Storeroom
10 Art room	

Bahia House

Salvador, Bahia, Brazil

Studio mk27 – Marcio Kogan,
Suzana Glogowski, Samanta Cafardo

Photography: Nelson Kon

Even when the sun is blazing and temperatures reach 40 °C (113 °F), the interior remains cool and airy without the need for artificial air conditioning.

A house doesn't have to be equipped with the latest hi-tech energy-saving gadgetry for it to be classed as energy efficient. There are more subtle, and natural, ways to conserve energy. Long before the invention of photovoltaic cells and geothermal heat pumps, traditional cultures had discovered how to build houses suited to, and which best took advantage of, their particular environment. Bahia House is a wonderful contemporary example of a house that draws on the traditional design wisdom of a Brazilian architecture specific to this region and passed down through generations of builders of bahian houses.

Located in Salvador, on Brazil's east coast, the house is designed to capitalise on the city's enviable climate, where even during winter temperatures rarely drop below 24 °C (75 °F). The exterior walls are sliding wooden lattice panels, which allow the house to literally open up to the lush central garden. Not only does this provide the residents with an intimate connection with nature, and a true outdoor/indoor living experience, the open design ensures effective cross-ventilation from the cooling northeastern sea breezes. Thus even when the sun is blazing and temperatures reach 40 °C (113 °F), the interior remains cool and airy without the need for artificial air conditioning. The clay roof, another feature of traditional bahian houses, harmonises beautifully with the surroundings, and is a fully recyclable and low embodied energy building material.

Modern advancements may have provided us with sophisticated technology to harness renewable energy and reduce carbon emissions, but we should never overlook simple and practical design principles that capitalise on local climatic characteristics. Bahia House is a beautiful reminder of this.

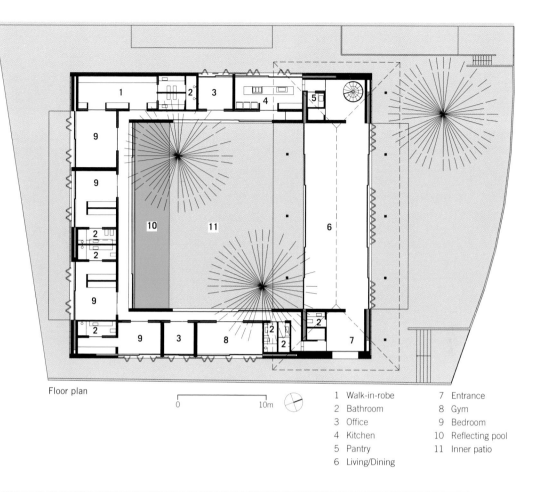

Floor plan

0   10m

1 Walk-in-robe
2 Bathroom
3 Office
4 Kitchen
5 Pantry
6 Living/Dining
7 Entrance
8 Gym
9 Bedroom
10 Reflecting pool
11 Inner patio

BC House

Monterrey, Nuevo León, Mexico

Gilberto L. Rodríguez, GLR Arquitectos

Photography: Jorge Taboada

Hidden beneath its cool modernist veil, BC House boasts some serious sustainability credentials.

With the rugged and imposing Sierra Madre mountain range as a backdrop, it is the style rather than the sustainability of BC House that first attracts one's attention. From the heaviness of the black granite, white exposed concrete and exposed steel elements, BC House is designed to evoke an image of lightness. But hidden beneath its cool modernist veil, its 'simple, pure geometric volumes', the house boasts some serious sustainability credentials, seamlessly blending stylish form with sustainability function.

Double walls with polyisocyanurate insulation and double-glazed windows with low-E glass reduce heat gain during Monterrey's long hot summers, when average temperatures hover around 35 °C (95 °F), significantly lowering the amount of energy required to cool the house. A green roof not only provides another layer of insulation, but displays a respect for the surroundings through an attempt to blend with the magnificent Sierra Madre Oriental mountain range in the distance.

Along with features designed to repel the sun are those to harness its energy. Both the hot water system and the swimming pool are solar heated, with south-facing skylights designed to provide natural sunlight and maximise solar gain during Monterrey's mild though relatively cool winters.

Monterrey's climate is classed as semi-arid, experiencing relatively low levels of annual rainfall. Water is thus a precious commodity that needs to be conserved and used responsibly. As a response to this, the BC House is equipped with a greywater treatment system for recycling grey water for irrigation, as well as a pluvial water system to catch and store rainwater. The xerisscape garden, designed to minimise water requirements, consists of hardy native plants adapted to Monterrey's low rainfall conditions.

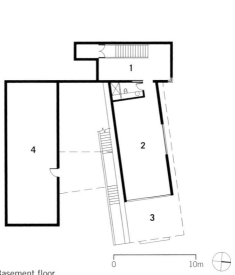

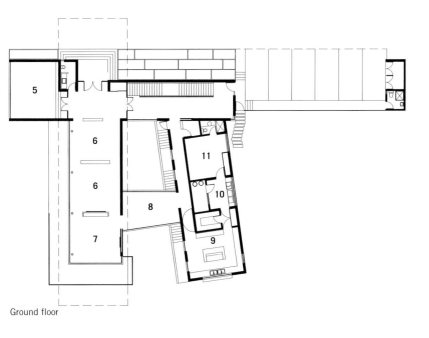

1 Foyer
2 Games room
3 Covered terrace
4 Garage
5 Library
6 Living
7 Dining
8 Breakfast room
9 Kitchen
10 Laundry
11 Service room
12 Bedroom
13 Inside patio
14 Machine room

Basement floor

0   10m

Ground floor

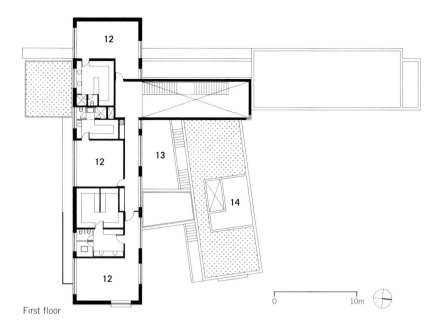

First floor

Big Dig House

Lexington, Massachusetts, USA

Single speed Design (SsD)

Photography: SsD

The Big Dig house is a literally concrete example of how to effectively reuse perfectly usable construction discards.

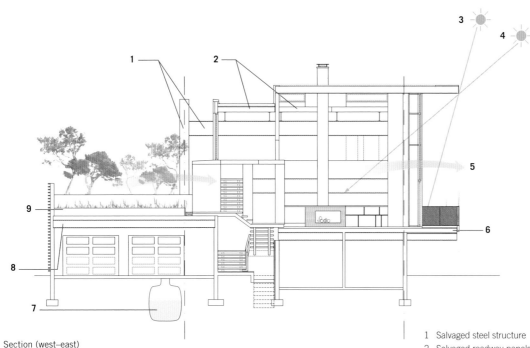

Section (west–east)

1 Salvaged steel structure
2 Salvaged roadway panels
3 Summer sun
4 Winter sun
5 Cross-ventilation
6 Salvaged roadway
 panels—thermal mass
 heated by sun
7 Salvaged cistern for
 watering roofscapes
8 Salvaged roadway panels
9 Roof garden with rainwater
 collection system

The structural system of the Big Dig house consists of approximately 272 tonnes (600,000 pounds) of steel and concrete salvaged from one of the United States' largest ever public works programs—Boston's Central Artery/Tunnel Project, otherwise known as the 'Big Dig'— which involved dismantling the city's elevated Central Artery (I-93), to be replaced by an underground highway.

The floors and lower roof consist of Inverset panels, 3-metre-wide (10-foot), 19-cm-thick (7.5-inch) reinforced concrete panels formerly used as temporary ramps and roadways during the Big Dig project, and which may well have ended up as landfill. The 31-tonne (69,000-pound) roof is braced by a 70-cm-thick (27-inch) painted girder, also salvaged from the project site. Even unearthed wooden marine piers, preserved after having been submerged for more than a century, were incorporated into the house's construction.

The substantial load-bearing capacity of the 'industrial strength' materials, stronger by far than materials typically used in house construction, ensured the lower roof could take the weight of a rooftop Japanese garden, as well as a second garden on the upper roof, not only improving insulation, and thus helping reduce energy consumption, but harvesting rainwater and reducing rain runoff.

Inside, window walls combined with double-height spaces allow natural light to penetrate deep into the interior, and are designed to harness the warmth of the winter sun.

The prefabricated nature of the recycled materials used also sped up the construction process, with the frame being put together in 12 hours instead of two weeks.

More than anything else, the Big Dig house is perhaps a prototype, a literally concrete example of how to effectively reuse perfectly usable construction discards that all too often end up as landfill. The house also points to larger-scale applications, with recycled major project materials an untapped potential source for the development of community programs such as schools, libraries and multi-residential complexes.

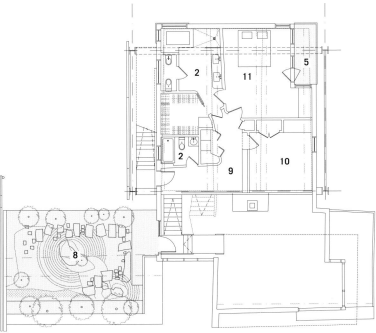

First floor

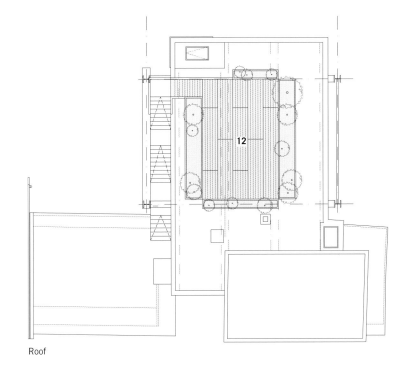

Roof

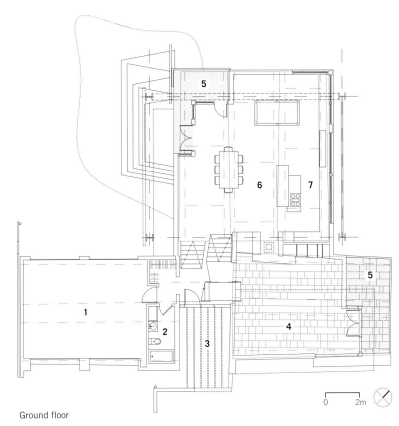

Ground floor

0   2m

1   Garage/Sculpture studio
2   Bathroom
3   Entry court
4   Great room
5   Terrace
6   Open living
7   Kitchen
8   Asian garden
9   Library
10 Office
11 Master bedroom
12 Roof garden

Big Dig House   37

Boano-Lowenstein Residence

Bay Harbor Islands, Florida, USA

Jaya Kader Zebede, AIA, LEED AP (KZ Architecture)

Photography: Robin Hill

The blending of modern and sustainable design was at the heart of the project from its inception.

The design excellence of the Boano-Lowenstein residence was recognised even before its construction, with KZ Architecture receiving the AIA Florida Unbuilt Merit Award for the house in 2008 then an award for Excellence in Architecture from the Miami chapter of the AIA once it was completed. The blending of modern and sustainable design was at the heart of the project from its inception, with both architect and owners enthusiastic about making sustainability a priority for this new home situated on an infill lot in Bay Harbor. Clear sustainable design goals were established at the outset by a team of environmentally minded and LEED-accredited professionals, with the result being not only a beautiful home that respects the character of the historic community, but one which has achieved LEED for Homes Silver Certification, Florida Green Building Coalition Gold Certification and a HERS score of 72.

The house is kept naturally cool under the hot Florida sun by the heat-resistant properties of the ceramic thermal block coating and bio-based spray-foam insulation. The high solar reflectance of the cool white roof also prevents heat penetrating the house. These features, along with 100 per cent solar-heated hot water and a 5650-litre cistern to store rainwater, have helped the house exceed the energy efficiency levels required by Florida's stringent building codes by 28 per cent, and reduced potable water usage by 45 per cent. More intrinsic sustainable elements include the use of regionally-sourced and environmentally-preferred construction materials, the use of low-VOC (Volatile Organic Compounds) or VOC-free paint throughout the house, natural light harvesting through the tubular sky lighting system, composite lumber decking, and the planting of native vegetation requiring minimal water.

The Boano-Lowenstein residence is an example of modern residential architecture respecting its local environment in an aesthetic sense and the global environment in a more profound sense.

First floor

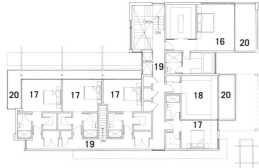

1	Entry gallery	12	Swimming
2	Living		pool
3	Dining/Family	13	Outdoor
4	Covered		kitchen
	terrace	14	Lawn
5	Kitchen	15	Dock
6	Service area	16	Master
7	Covered entry		bedroom
	path	17	Bedroom
8	Courtyard	18	Library
9	Lily pond	19	Gallery
10	Garage	20	Balcony
11	Motor court		

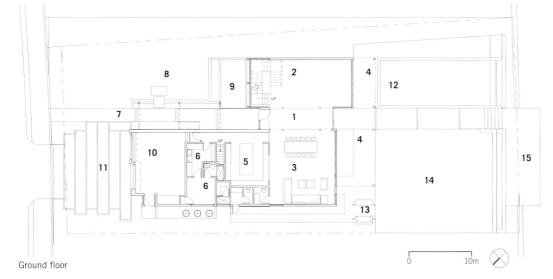

Ground floor

0   10m

Bungalow @ 5 Polo Club

Kota Damansara, Selangor, Malaysia

Masyerin M.N. Architect

Photography: Joe Low (Photics Productions),
Tan Tek Tsien (MMN Design)

The orientation and allocation of spaces was determined by the path of the sun and the direction of prevailing winds.

Bungalow @ 5 Polo Club is a modern interpretation of a traditional Malay *kampung* ('village') house, built specifically for Malaysia's hot and humid tropical climate. The year-round average maximum temperature hovers around 27 °C (80 °F) to 30 °C (86 °F), with the average minimum temperature not much lower. Keeping a house cool and comfortable is therefore an important concern.

The house was conceived as a series of 'screens' that visually partition the house and control public and private views, dividing the home into three different 'zones'—private, semi-public and public. The 'green zone', or courtyard, at the middle of the site is the central focus of the home, a common area onto which all rooms open.

The orientation and allocation of spaces in this house was determined by the path of the sun and the direction of prevailing winds to maximise the effectiveness of natural ventilation and at the same time maximise the level of natural light into areas of the building that require it the most. To this end, internal spaces are arranged to open up towards the north and south, while the slim U-shaped building form is designed to optimise natural daylighting and ventilation.

The façades facing east and west have deep overhangs and minimal openings in order to minimise heat gain due to the low-angle morning and evening sun. The swimming pool in the central 'green space' courtyard also acts as an evaporative cooling system. The consumption of energy is significantly reduced through this relatively simple form of passive cooling and daylighting.

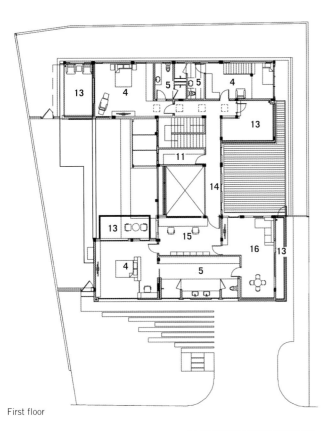

First floor

1 Garden	9 Kitchen
2 Patio	10 Living
3 Courtyard	11 Store room
4 Bedroom	12 Carport
5 Bathroom	13 Balcony
6 Lap pool	14 Gallery
7 Patio	15 Study
8 Dining	16 TV room

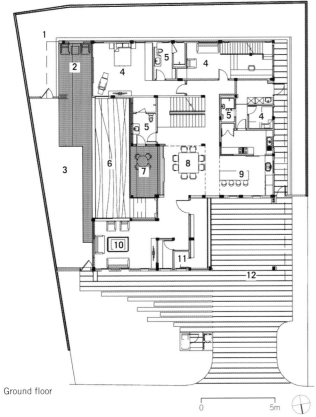

Ground floor

0   5m

Cedeira House

Cedeira, Galicia, Spain

MYCC Architecture

Photography: Fernando Guerra, FG+SG

The environmental benefits of prefabricated houses commence at the production stage.

The increasing demand for sustainable homes, or at least homes with elements of sustainability, has seen a resurgence in the popularity of prefabricated, or modular, homes, once disparaged as cheap, mass-produced carbon-copy kit homes. But this image has undergone significant reevaluation in recent years, not least because of interesting designs like Cedeira House. The benefits of prefabricated houses are gradually being appreciated, and not just their often cheaper price tag and significantly reduced construction times.

The environmental benefits of prefabricated houses commence at the production stage. The controlled factory environment in which the sections of the prefab house are manufactured generally involves less waste than with traditional onsite construction methods, due to the precision and efficiencies achieved via the mass production process. On a large scale, the one-off delivery of completed modules to the construction site can also involve a reduction in emissions from transportation to and from the site typical with standard home construction. On-site noise pollution levels are also minimised by the shortened construction times.

Located in Cedeira, a small tourist and fishing town in the northwest of Spain, this holiday house consists of six modules, approximately 6 metres (20 feet) long and 3 metres (10 feet) wide, manufactured in three months and constructed in three days, involving little environmental disturbance to its beautiful site on the northeast corner of the Iberian Peninsula, with its sweeping ocean views. The tree silhouettes cut into the house's Cor-ten cladding not only provide an interesting natural daylight display, but blend harmoniously with the slender eucalypt forest in the background and the surrounding harvest fields. Cor-ten itself was chosen because of it relationship to the traditions of the region's fishing villages, used for the construction of boat hulls, while its patina and changing colour creates a lively image that relates with the natural environment.

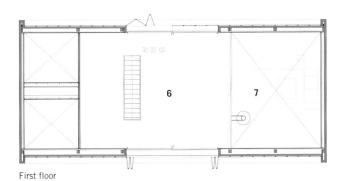

First floor

Ground floor

1 Bedroom
2 Corridor
3 Bathroom
4 Kitchen
5 Living
6 Loft
7 Void

0   5m

Christie Beach Residence

Christie Beach, Ontario, Canada

Altius Architecture

Photography: Patrick Burke

West-facing windows are designed to harvest natural daylight and the warmth of the afternoon winter sun, while the heat mirror glazing provides shading and insulation.

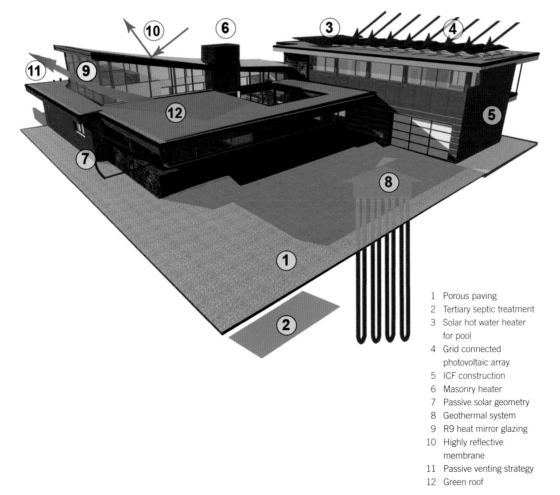

1 Porous paving
2 Tertiary septic treatment
3 Solar hot water heater for pool
4 Grid connected photovoltaic array
5 ICF construction
6 Masonry heater
7 Passive solar geometry
8 Geothermal system
9 R9 heat mirror glazing
10 Highly reflective membrane
11 Passive venting strategy
12 Green roof

As its starting point, the aim of the design of the Christie Beach residence was to minimise its impact on the environment and harmonise with the surrounding landscape. It does this aesthetically with its rich red cedar and cherry woods and stone exterior contrasting wonderfully against the green of the forest during summer. Further integration with the site was achieved by setting the building low and shifting floor and roof planes to physically embed the spaces into the landscape. Passive and active elements have been deftly incorporated into the design of the house so that function and form blend seamlessly, unifying building, occupant and landscape.

West-facing windows are designed to harvest natural daylight and the warmth of the afternoon winter sun, while the heat mirror glazing provides shading and insulation. Internal temperatures are naturally regulated via large internal thermal mass and cross-ventilation through the wide sliding glass doors positioned at the north and south of the house, with stack ventilation and

passive venting acting as a natural cooling mechanism. The locally-sourced limestone and wood, and an ICF construction with spray-applied polyurethane, acts as a thermally-resistant envelope. Further insulation is provided by an expansive green roof, and a highly reflective roof membrane reduces heat penetration during the warmer months.

Active systems are used to supplement passive measures when required. A vertical ground-loop geothermal system is used as the primary heating system, backed up by a clean woodburning contraflow masonry stove. Electricity use is offset by a 10-kilowatt grid-connected photovoltaic array, while a solar hot water system is used to heat the pool.

The house's striking form nevertheless blends seamlessly with its environment, the result of considered material choice and thoughtful design. Rich and warm, this sustainable home combines comfort and environmental conscientiousness.

1 Living
2 Dining
3 Kitchen
4 Recreation
5 Study
6 Master bedroom
7 Service
8 Courtyard
9 Garage
10 Bedroom
11 W.C.
12 Loft
13 Green roof

Ground floor

0   6m

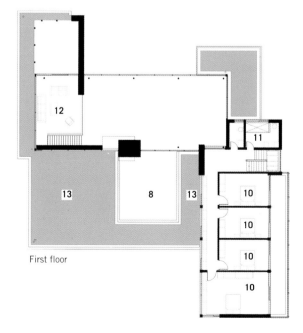

First floor

CO$_2$-Saver

Lake Laka, Silesia, Poland

Peter Kuczia

Photography: Tomek Pikula and Peter Kuczia

A sustainable house need not cost more than a conventional one.

The relatively expensive technology often associated with energy-efficient design has linked sustainability with high upfront costs. Yet the CO$_2$-Saver, located in the Upper Silesian region of Poland, shows that a sustainable house need not cost more than a conventional one.

This compact house, constructed of a blend of locally sourced recycled and recyclable materials, is designed to maximise solar gain, with roughly 80 per cent of the building envelope facing the sun, over 10 per cent more exposure than a traditionally designed house. The south-facing glass atrium, with angled glazed roof panels, enables natural light to flood in and absorbs the warmth from the sun, creating a winter garden effect, while opening up in summer to take advantage of the warm breeze.

Solar panels positioned above the atrium are used for heating water. According to the architect, they heat about 30 to 40 per cent of the hot water used during winter, and 100 per cent during summer. Emerging above the solar

panels is the three-storey 'black box', clad with charcoal-coloured fibre cement panels with high thermal mass, designed to minimise heat loss. A green roof sits on either side of the black box, providing further insulation and harmony with the surroundings. The house's timber cladding is made from locally sourced and untreated larchwood, the panels placed slightly apart to facilitate circulation.

Inside, the walls are insulated naturally with loam, and building material is conserved through the simple polished concrete floor, which also has high thermal mass. Ventilation is provided by the home's thermal recovery ventilation system, which maintains the room temperature while enabling fresh outside air to flow in, warmed by the leftover heat of the expelled indoor air passing out through ducts.

Integral to the design of CO$_2$-Saver was the minimisation of both construction costs and lifecycle running costs, achieved through simple but well thought out design.

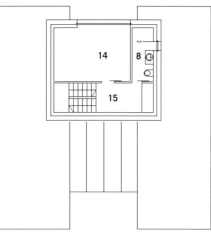

Top floor

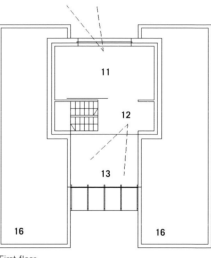

First floor

1 Living
2 Dining
3 Kitchen
4 Storage
5 Porch
6 Wardrobe
7 Laundry
8 Bathroom
9 Bedroom
10 Terrace
11 Studio
12 Gallery
13 Patio
14 Room with view onto lake
15 Corridor
16 Green roof

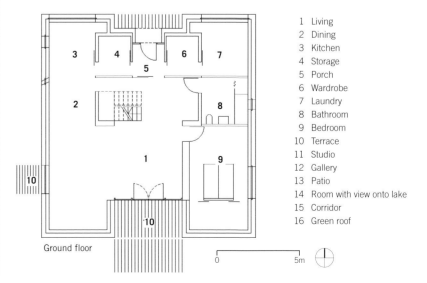

Ground floor

0   5m

Courtyard House

Los Angeles, California, USA

Thomas Robertson (principal), Ripple Design

Photography: Marla Aufmuth

Photovoltaic panels harness more than enough solar energy to power the house, with the excess electricity being fed back into the grid.

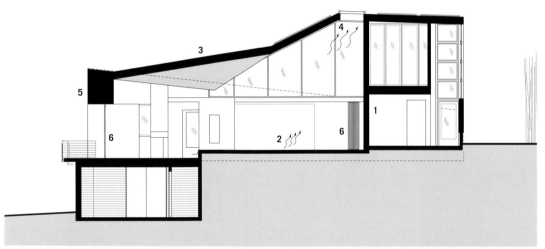

Passive Section

1 Thermal mass
2 Radiant heated floor
3 Reflective roof
4 Thermal chimney
5 Calculated roof overhead
6 Fully retractable door
   systems

The focus on sustainability in the design of Courtyard House is evident in an array of passive and active sustainable design elements. Located only a few miles inland from the Pacific Ocean, the house is positioned to collect and distribute the cooling westerly breezes, which can then be regulated via the fully retractable doors that surround the central courtyard. Inside, the sloping roof helps circulate the air through the thermal chimney effect, in which the naturally rising warmer air creates an upward airflow.

The galvanised steel roof reflects the heat of the hot California sun, while roof angles and strategically placed overhangs are designed to minimise solar gain in summer while benefiting from the warmth in winter. Photovoltaic panels harness more than enough solar energy to power the house, with the excess electricity being fed back into the grid. Household water is heated via solar panels, which also provide the energy source for the radiant floor heating system, backed up by an on-demand gas boiler.

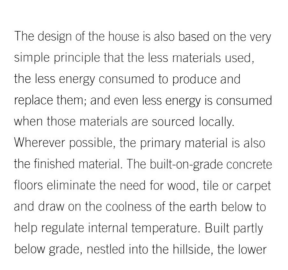

First floor

1 Mechanical room
2 Storeroom
3 Lower courtyard
4 Garage
5 Study
6 Dark room
7 Living
8 Foyer
9 Bathroom
10 Balcony
11 Upper courtyard
12 Dining
13 Bedroom
14 Den
15 Kitchen
16 Breakfast nook
17 Hall
18 Laundry

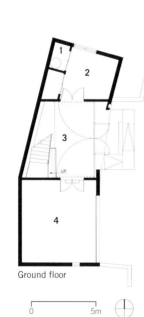

Ground floor

0   5m

The design of the house is also based on the very simple principle that the less materials used, the less energy consumed to produce and replace them; and even less energy is consumed when those materials are sourced locally. Wherever possible, the primary material is also the finished material. The built-on-grade concrete floors eliminate the need for wood, tile or carpet and draw on the coolness of the earth below to help regulate internal temperature. Built partly below grade, nestled into the hillside, the lower level also benefits from the earth's natural cooling. The house's untreated stucco exterior further adds to its thermal mass.

Sustainability principles have been applied at all stages of the design and construction of Courtyard House, a house whose sense of openness strives to embrace the environment and the surrounding community at the same time.

Dalkeith House

Dalkeith, Western Australia, Australia

Iredale Pedersen Hook Architects

Photography: Peter Bennetts

Dalkeith House seeks to deny the contemporary and popular image of what a sustainable house should look like.

This house, located in the old Perth suburb of Dalkeith and surrounded by the Swan River on three sides, embraces a design that seeks to deny the contemporary and popular image of what a sustainable house should look like. The collection of low-tech, cost-effective sustainable design features is bound by this architectural intent, which adopts the elements of platform, pavilions and parasols in its exploration of the relationship between house and garden.

Perth is the third windiest city in the world, and the design of Dalkeith House makes the most of the freshening southwesterly breezes that blow in from the Indian Ocean. The pavilions are articulated to allow wind to penetrate deep in to the house after being cooled by shallow ponds adjacent to the low-level windows, while hot air is drawn from the house through the top windows. The articulated form increases the roof area and therefore its water catchment capacity. Captured water is stored in sub-surface concrete tanks that supply both the pool and house. Water is heated by a solar hot water system with back-up gas instantaneous heater and solar-heated roof-mounted pipes. Water consumption is minimised through low flow fittings, and the entire house is prepared for blackwater recycling (when local legislation permits this form of recycling).

Roof-mounted photovoltaic cells provide power, while consumption is minimised via compact and T5 fluorescent light fittings and low-energy fixtures. The photovoltaic cells, parasol roof and hot water system shade the roof to reduce heat build-up. Winter heating is provided by direct sun thermal heat gain on the concrete platform, supplemented with ethanol fireplaces and sub-surface pipes.

The house is constructed of plantation pine, and the cantilevers with plantation plywood. The use of steel and other high-embodied energy materials is minimised. It is clad in a composite fire rated panel with sheet steel exterior and an acid-free recyclable core, providing superior thermal performance and minimal material waste.

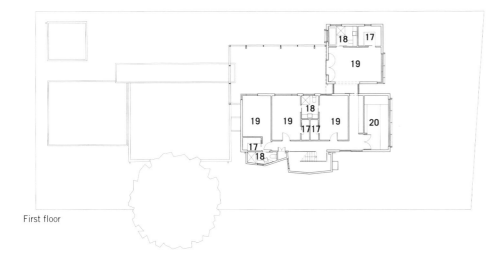

First floor

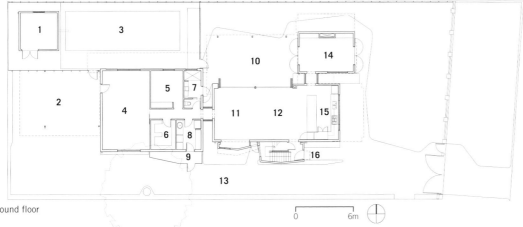

Ground floor

0   6m

1   Storeroom/Workshop
2   Carport/Party area
3   Pool
4   Games room
5   Guest bedroom
6   Wine store
7   Bathroom
8   Laundry
9   Services court
10 Outdoor living
11 Living
12 Dining
13 Playing field
14 Lounge
15 Kitchen
16 Entry
17 Wardrobe
18 Ensuite
19 Bedroom
20 Study

DT House

Oeiras, Portugal

Jorge Graça Costa

Photography: FG+SG

Air cooled by the evaporation of the water is moved through the house via the freshening southerly breezes from the Atlantic.

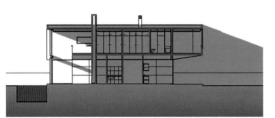

Solar heating

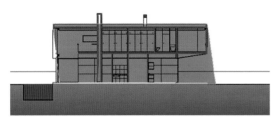

Solar shading

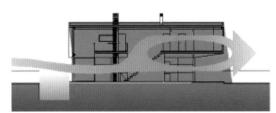

Natural ventilation and evaporative cooling

This relatively compact house sited on a hill overlooking the Atlantic Ocean is another example of how, in the right climate, energy efficiencies can be achieved through simple passive design features without requiring more complex, energy-consuming mechanical systems.

Material salvaged from the demolition of the dilapidated pre-existing house was used as part of the foundations for DT House. Material was also recycled for use in the concrete pathway and outdoor courtyard. All non-recycled materials used in the construction were chosen based on their durability and potential for future reuse and recycling. Cork, for example, has been used for floor insulation in the upper level.

The south-facing side of the house basically consists of two levels of floor-to-ceiling double-glazed windows that harness and retain heat from the winter sun while at the same time providing plenty of natural light. The design prevents solar gain during the summer. Beyond its typical uses and the stunning visual element it brings to the house, the strategically-positioned pool is designed to act as a natural evaporative cooling system. The air cooled by the evaporation of the water is moved through the house via the freshening southerly breezes from the Atlantic, circulating air through the two levels of the house. The completely natural process (the pool water is chemical-free) is so effective and so efficient the house uses four times less energy than a typical Portuguese house for cooling during summer. The water can also be used for irrigation purposes.

DT House is architecture adapted to make best use of the natural advantages of the Oeiras climate, with its generally mild winters and warm to hot summers. Designed with intelligence and foresight, this stylish, minimalist house blends perfectly with its surroundings and demonstrates the effectiveness of simple passive strategies.

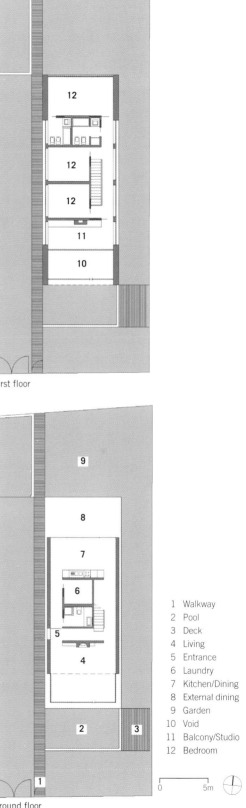

First floor

Ground floor

1 Walkway
2 Pool
3 Deck
4 Living
5 Entrance
6 Laundry
7 Kitchen/Dining
8 External dining
9 Garden
10 Void
11 Balcony/Studio
12 Bedroom

0   5m

DT House   69

El Ray House

Dungeness Beach, Kent, UK

Simon Conder Associates

Photography: Chris Gascoigne

It is anticipated that the wind turbine will generate more electricity during the year than the house will consume.

El Ray is part of a group of five beach houses located immediately to the east of the huge Dungeness A power station. The original house consisted of a 19th-century railway carriage with flimsy lean-tos to the north and south. Due to planning restrictions which require any 'new' house in the area to be seen as an 'extension' to an existing structure, it was both necessary and desirable to retain the original railway carriage, which has been incorporated as a free-standing object inside a new highly insulated timber structure, forming the centre point of the main living area.

Temperature control is achieved through a combination of super insulation, passive solar gain, cross ventilation and a wind turbine.

The high levels of insulation in the walls, roof and floor ensure that heat loss from the building is minimal and very little energy is required for heating, lighting and ventilation. External glazing consists of a combination of double-glazed, low-E, argon-filled frameless fixed lights and thermally-broken aluminium sliding doors. The structural timber frame is constructed from light-weight engineered timber I-Joists, braced inside and out with a sheathing material manufactured entirely from wood waste. The insulation between the I-joists and studs is made from recycled newspaper. The external cladding and decking is made of an FSC-certified hardwood called itauba, and the internal wall linings, floors and all joinery are constructed of FSC-certified birch plywood.

A canopy projects out over the south deck to shade the living areas from the high summer sun, but allows the low winter sun to warm the house. When necessary a wood-burning stove, using drift wood from the beach, is used to supplement the passive solar gain in the winter months, and in extremely cold conditions electric underfloor heating, powered by the wind turbine, will heat the two bedrooms and the bathroom.

It is anticipated that the wind turbine will generate more electricity during the year than the house will consume, making the house carbon negative and producing excess electricity that can be sold back into the national grid.

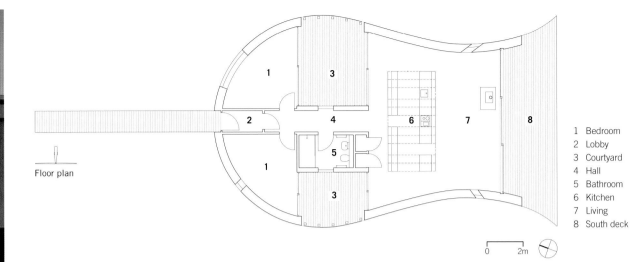

Floor plan

1 Bedroom
2 Lobby
3 Courtyard
4 Hall
5 Bathroom
6 Kitchen
7 Living
8 South deck

0   2m

English Residence

Orleans, Massachusetts, USA

ZeroEnergy Design

Photography: Michael J Lee

A green roof not only provides added insulation but further connects the house with the environment.

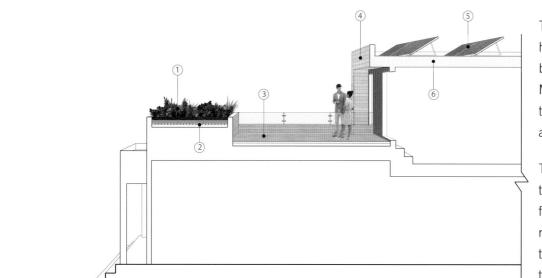

1 Green roof
2 Reclaimed wood
3 FSC-certified timber decking
4 Window shading
5 Solar panels
6 Roof and wall insulation

The English residence replaces a seasonal house originally built in 1958 in the popular beachside holiday area of Cape Cod in Massachusetts. The new house is a product of the owners' strong environmental philosophy and their love of the outdoors.

The house consists of three delineated forms— the 'orange box' and the 'red box' on the ground floor (the autumnal colour palette designed to reflect the changing colour of the leaves), with the first-floor 'cedar box' positioned to give shade to the orange box's south-facing windows, preventing solar heat gain during summer but allowing in the warming rays from the lower winter sun. The red box's south-facing windows are shaded by mature deciduous trees that provide shade in the summer and sun in the winter when their leaves have fallen. The high-performance building envelope consists of spray foam insulation and rigid insulation, equipping the house with a tight wall free of thermal bridging. A green roof not only provides added insulation but further connects the house with

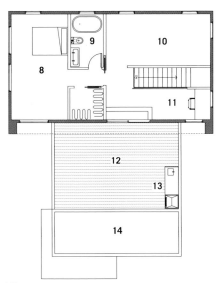

First floor

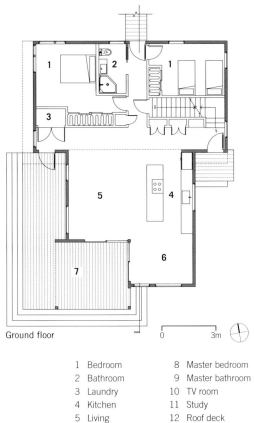

Ground floor

0   3m

1 Bedroom	8 Master bedroom
2 Bathroom	9 Master bathroom
3 Laundry	10 TV room
4 Kitchen	11 Study
5 Living	12 Roof deck
6 Dining	13 Outdoor kitchen
7 Covered porch	14 Green roof

the environment, also giving the first-floor deck area a pleasant, tranquil garden space.

Energy-efficient heating is provided by a high-efficiency condensing boiler and radiant floor heating. Indoor air quality is maintained with an allergen filtration system and a heat recovery ventilator, which provides fresh air while minimising energy losses by exchanging heat between incoming and outgoing air streams. One third of the home's electricity use is offset by photovoltaic panels. Combined, these sustainability features yielded the house a HERS score of 39, which means the house uses roughly 60 per cent less energy than a code-built equivalent home.

Many sustainable materials were also used in the construction of the house, including bamboo flooring, recycled tile, quartz countertops, fibre-cement and cedar siding, FSC-certified decking, reclaimed decking, and low-VOC paints, earning the house LEED for Homes Gold certification.

Gap House

London, UK

Pitman Tozer Architects

Photography: Nick Kane

The main challenge posed by the narrow site was to create a comfortable four-bedroom family home that maximised light and minimised carbon emissions.

Sited on a plot only 2.4 metres (8 feet) wide, this terraced London townhouse proves that sustainable architecture is achievable without compromise on the tightest of urban sites. The main challenge posed by the narrow, awkward site, originally the side alley and rear garden of an adjoining property, was to create a comfortable four-bedroom family home that maximised light and minimised carbon emissions.

To provide each habitable room with sufficient light and a sense of spaciousness, even within the narrowest part of the building, the smaller bedrooms are stacked at the front of the house, facing the street, while the rear is organised in a cascading configuration, with the wet rooms and storage areas occupying those parts of the house that receive no natural light. A courtyard at the rear of the site brings light into the ground floor reception space, while a central twisting timber stair brings daylight deep into the centre of the plan on each floor.

The walls and roof of the house are highly insulated, using natural materials wherever possible, such as lamb's wool for the internal walls. Heating requirements are further reduced through the maximisation of solar gain. High-performance, low-energy windows with timber frames made from sustainable spruce further reduce energy use.

Three 50-metre-deep bore holes were dug below the rear courtyard, serving a 12-kilowatt ground coupled heat pump installed in the plant room, which provides all the heating (underfloor) and hot water for the house. Water consumption is minimised through a rainwater harvesting system designed specifically to suit the constrained nature of the site, with recycled water used to flush the toilets.

As well as bringing light into the property, the geometrically complex self-supporting stair acts as a four-storey stack for passive ventilation in the summer.

Winner of the 2009 Manser Medal, Gap House is designed to use approximately 40 per cent of the energy of a typical house built to current UK building regulations. A recent in-house post-completion assessment rated the house as Grade 4 (Exemplary) under the UK Code for Sustainable Homes.

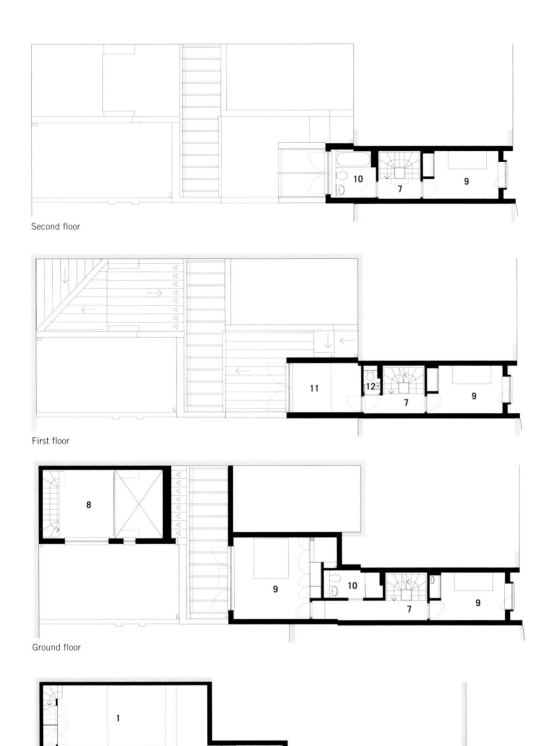

Second floor

First floor

Ground floor

Lower ground floor

1 Living
2 Courtyard
3 Dining
4 Kitchen
5 Utility room
6 Plant room
7 Hall
8 Study
9 Bedroom
10 Bathroom
11 Conservatory
12 W.C.

0   3m

Hill End Ecohouse

Hill End, Queensland, Australia

Riddel Architecture

Photography: Christopher Frederick Jones

Roughly 75 per cent of the house is constructed from recycled materials.

Sustainability is at the very core of the design and construction of the Hill End Ecohouse, with all design features, materials and products rigorously assessed for their environmental, social and economic sustainability credentials. Roughly 75 per cent of the house is constructed from recycled materials sourced from the original 1930s house it replaced, nearby salvage yards and new products containing recycled content. The remainder of material used was sourced as locally as possible and selected for its low environmental impact.

The open design of the house caters for an outdoor lifestyle suited to Brisbane's subtropical climate, with its hot summers and mild winters. The central courtyard allows winter sunshine into the rear living spaces, filling rooms with natural light, and captures cooling summer breezes that then circulate through the house. Wood-framed operable glass walls add to this sense of openness and promote natural ventilation. This passive form of cooling, combined with efficient insulation and the thermal mass of the concrete floors and walls, is so effective the house doesn't require an air conditioning system.

The house is entirely self-sufficient in terms of water and electricity needs. Underground tanks with a combined capacity of 70,000 litres store enough harvested rainwater for the house, garden and pool. Harvested rainwater for general household use is filtered first, then again for higher grade drinking water in the kitchen.

Water is heated with solar panels, and a hot water recirculating unit diverts warming water in showers from waste pipes to storage tanks until the water runs hot. Salvaged water is treated and reused on site. A 3.2-kilowatt photovoltaic array on the north-facing roof generates more than enough energy for the house's daily electricity requirements. To further improve energy efficiency, an internal monitoring system keeps track of electricity, gas and water usage.

With its high ratio of recycled materials and combined active and passive sustainable design features, the Hill End Ecohouse is an eminently liveable example of how household carbon energy requirements can be effectively neutralised without any sacrifice of comfort.

Second floor

Trellis structure with vegetation for shading

3.2 kW solar array

Solar hot water unit

Tank pre-filter unit

First floor

45,000-litre underground rainwater tanks (household supply)

Greywater treatment (irrigation, toilets, washing machine)

25,000-litre permeable underground water storage (irrigation and pool)

Ground floor

Solar power invertor, rainwater pumps and water filters

0   4m

1 Garage
2 Entry
3 Plant room
4 Cellar
5 Media room
6 Hall
7 Bedroom
8 W.C. and shower
9 Gym
10 Pool
11 Balcony
12 Bathroom
13 Laundry
14 Study
15 Courtyard
16 Gallery
17 Dining
18 Kitchen
19 River terrace
20 Living
21 Walk-in-robe

House 205

Vacarisses, Catalonia, Spain

H Arquitectes

Photography: Starp Estudi, Anna Bonet

The design minimised materials required for the foundations, translating into reduced embodied energy and associated carbon emissions.

A lot of care was taken in the construction of House 205 to do as little environmental damage to the site as possible. To minimise excavation work, two concrete struts were used as the foundations for the rectangular-shaped house, fixed to a natural rocky platform and creating a ventilated space between the floor and the rocky ground. In addition to causing minimal disruption to the land, the layout was chosen to enable a more efficient dimensioning of the structure using large arches that articulate the geometry of the rock and the house. The design minimised materials required for the foundations, translating into reduced embodied energy and associated carbon emissions. The use of low-weight laminated wood panels enabled the diffusion of weight as though the structure was a single beam. The house was also constructed in an efficient 'dry assembly' process that

requires far less water than traditional house construction. The interior floor, ceiling and walls are lined with fully recyclable laminated wooden panels that can be reused if the house is ever dimantled. Solar energy is collected by the solar panels positioned on the south-facing façade.

Taking into consideration embodied energy and energy consumed for heating, ventilation, air conditioning, domestic hot water, lighting and domestic electrical appliances, it is estimated that over a period of 50 years House 205 will produce 51 per cent less carbon emissions than a standard house[1]. It is this kind of energy efficiency that saw this compact 132-square-metre (1421-square-foot) house awarded the Sustainable Architecture Award 2009 at the 5th Valles Architecture Biennial.

1   Data from the research 'Factor 10. Reduction of CO_2'.
    Authors: Joan Sabaté – SaaS – Jordina Vidal

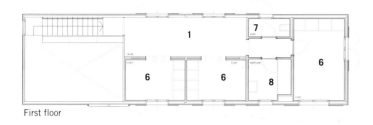

First floor

Ground floor

0   5m

1   Study/Studio
2   Living
3   Laundry
4   Kitchen
5   Pantry
6   Bedroom
7   Bath
8   Bathroom

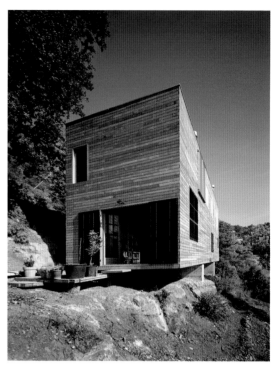

House Among the Pines

Montepinar, Murcia, Spain

Javier Peña Galiano

Photography: Jesús Granada

The polyhedron-shaped structure, with its green-blue iridescent cladding, reflects and blends in with the surrounding pines.

House Among the Pines's steep, rocky site was not the easiest of locations to build a house on, but wherever possible these difficulties were transformed into benefits. The design of the house was born of a desire to highlight the natural beauty of the Mediterranean forest in which it is located. The resulting polyhedron-shaped structure, with its green-blue iridescent cladding, reflects and blends in with the surrounding pines.

A lot of the natural material existing on the site was recovered and incorporated into the building. Stone from the plot was used for retaining walls, salvaged timber was used for the wooden pathways, and a replacement tree was planted for every tree salvaged from the site during the building of the house.

Built partly into the mountainside, the house makes use of the earth's consistent temperature as a natural form of insulation; and to conserve energy, all rooms that don't require natural light were placed in this lower level area. Another layer of insulation is provided by the thermo-clay within the sandwich panels that clad the house. Rainwater captured from the roof is used for irrigation.

A grassy courtyard is situated beneath the suspended upper level of the house, inviting in breezes to circulate through the house and creating a shaded outdoor area that remains cool on even the hottest days. Wide east- and south-facing windows let in natural light, while the heat mirroring film within the double-glazed glass reduces solar gain. A sophisticated louvre system covering some of the windows provides automatically controlled shading from the sun.

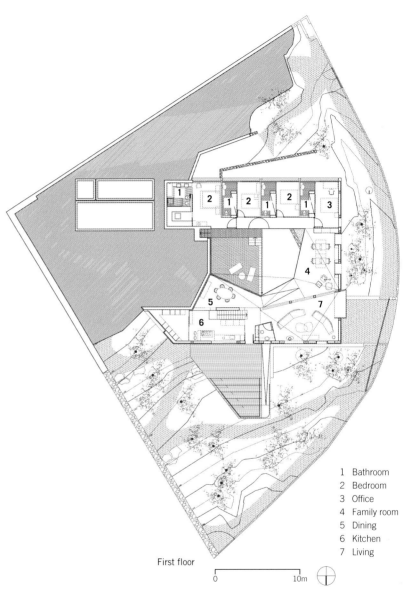

1 Bathroom
2 Bedroom
3 Office
4 Family room
5 Dining
6 Kitchen
7 Living

First floor

0   10m

House in Matsubara

Setagaya, Tokyo, Japan

Satoshi Okada

Photography: Hiroyuki Hirai

In summer, the front garden is heated by direct sunlight while the rear garden remains shaded and cool.

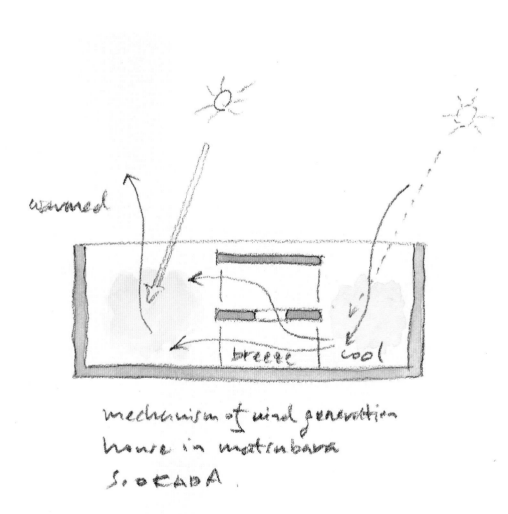

warmed

breeze   cool

mechanism of wind generation
house in matsubara
S. OKADA.

Even if love, respect and awareness of nature was not such a fundamental part of Japanese culture, the combination of very limited natural resources, a large population and relatively small land mass would have encouraged the efficient use of space and energy.

The design of this house in a typical residential district of Tokyo blends contemporary practice with the wisdom of the *machiya* (traditional wooden townhouse), a form of housing once common in the historical capital of Kyoto. Typically these were long, narrow wooden houses with one or more courtyard gardens helping maintain a comfortable temperature on even the hottest summer day.

House in Matsubara, with its main living section enclosed by a concrete wall, contains a front and rear garden. The front garden functions as a tiny tea garden. Traditionally one accessed these tea gardens via a *roji* ('dewy path'), which symbolised the first step in breaking from the bustle of the outside world. In summer, the front

First floor

2

1

Ground floor

1 Carport
2 Entrance gate
3 Garden for tearoom
4 Entrance
5 Bathroom
6 Tearoom
7 Hall
8 Closet/Storage
9 Master bedroom
10 Rear garden
11 W.C.
12 Terrace
13 Living
14 Dining/Kitchen

0   2m

garden is heated by direct sunlight while the rear garden remains shaded and cool. As the heat rises in the front garden, the cooler air is pulled from the rear garden, travelling down the hall that connects the two gardens and passively cooling the house without the need for an air conditioner except on exceptionally hot days. It is a very simple and yet very effective design that also provides the house with a tranquil green space. In winter, the heat absorbed and then radiated by the concrete wall warms the living area.

Construction time was reduced radically by implementing the Light-steel Panel Unit System (LsPUS) – a structural method developed by the architect. The use of light-steel panel units instead of standard reinforced concrete panels resulted in a construction period of just a few days instead of months. The panels can also be dismantled and rearranged/reused, making this Japanese house one that embraces both traditional and contemporary principles of sustainability.

House in the Forest

Valle de Bravo, Mexico State, Mexico

Parque Humano, Jorge Covarrubias and Benjamin Gonzalez

Photography: Paul Rivera, ArchPhoto

Trees were incorporated into the design to highlight the house's connection with and respect for nature.

If we are permitted to use the term 'sustainability' in a fuller, broader sense, focusing not just on technical concepts like embodied energy levels but incorporating a building's physical and aesthetic relationship with its immediate surroundings, then House in the Forest is a very beautiful example of how lightly a house can impact on its surroundings and how well it can blend with its natural environment.

Located near Avándaro Lake and the protected forest area of Cerro Gordo, rich with pine and oak trees, the philosophy behind the design of the house was to respect nature to the fullest and forge a connection with its surroundings, and by its very existence generate that same respect for the natural world.

While average maximum temperatures hover between 20 °C (68 °F) and 30 °C (86 °F) in the Valle de Bravo area, approximately 150 kilometres (93 miles) southwest of Mexico City, it can reach as high as 33 °C (91 °F) in summer and as low as –2 °C (24 °F) in winter, a temperature range the design of the house needed to accomodate.

The house rests on a natural ledge in the hillside, its elevation providing expansive views of the nearby lake and mountain range beyond. Large floor-to-ceiling south-facing windows receive the warmth from the winter sun, while the overhangs from the angled ceiling offer shade from the harsh summer sun. The north façade blocks the strong northerly winds.

No trees were removed during the construction of the house, and many were incorporated into the design to highlight the house's connection with and respect for nature. A special form of clay with natural insulation properties was developed for the cladding, similar in texture to that used for traditional houses found in the area, so that the house would fit in with the context of the town. All timber and stone used in the construction was locally sourced, rainwater is captured and stored and greywater reused, and solar panels generate most of the household's electricity needs.

With its earthy tones and textures, shrouded by the trees so respected by its design, House in the Forest sits so lightly on the hillside it seems almost to fade into it.

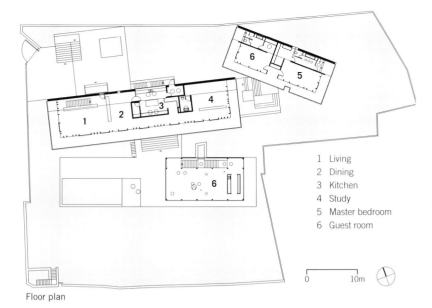

Floor plan

1 Living
2 Dining
3 Kitchen
4 Study
5 Master bedroom
6 Guest room

0   10m

House in the Forest

House Reduction

Dublin, Ireland

Solearth Ecological Architecture

Photography: Ros Kavanagh

Materials salvaged from the original structure were used extensively in the remodelling.

The concept of a house *extension* is a familiar one, but not so much a house reduction. But with increased energy costs making it more and more expensive to heat and cool what are often unnecessarily large houses, not to mention the waste of energy this entails, perhaps it is a trend that will catch on.

The impetus for this redesign of a semi-detached house was the reduction in space required by a shrinking family and a desire to generally improve 'liveability'. What resulted was the removal of the ground-floor bedroom and two walls of the kitchen, in part to create a light-filled 'window' room which flows visually and, in certain window configurations, spatially into the garden. The redesign also incorporated a utility room, larder, reconfigured bathroom and outside deck, or courtyard, and elegant formal pool. Materials salvaged from the original structure were used extensively in the remodelling.

The addition of glass sliding doors has not only opened up the house to the outdoors, but has increased the level of natural light and ventilation through the house. The new clerestory window is a further source of natural light. Heat is retained within the house through the single leaf thermal honeycomb block insulation in the new walls. Water for the formal pool is supplied by harvested rainwater, and water is now heated by a series of solar panels that line the roof.

Though the size of the house has been reduced, the optimised use of space and a clever design that opens the house up and connects it with the garden outside makes it feel larger, roomier, and certainly more energy-efficient.

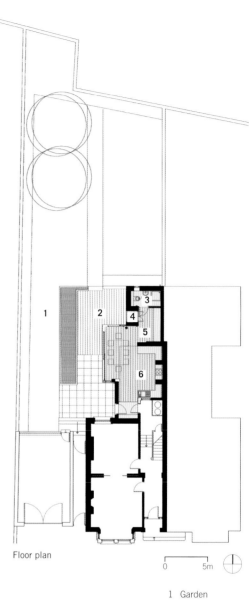

Floor plan

0   5m

1 Garden
2 Deck
3 Bathroom
4 Pantry
5 Utility
6 Kitchen/Dining

House Ulve

Varsatie, Seinäjoki, Finland

Lassila Hirvilammi Architects

Photography: Jussi Tiainen

The openings and blinds work together, allowing freshening breezes to circulate while blocking out the summer sun.

Located in the old rural district of Seinäjoki, in Finland, House Ulve is a blend of two different architectural traditions, containing elements of a typical Finnish *pohjalaistalo*, or farmhouse, and a classic Norwegian fisherman's cottage. To blend in with the smaller scale of the surrounding predominantly 1950s-era housing, the relatively large house was split into two connecting volumes.

The living room, dining room and kitchen are placed in the street-facing side of the house, while the bedrooms and other auxiliary spaces are located in the second, double-storey volume. The resulting L-shape design creates a convenient 'inner court micro-climate'. The openings and blinds work together, allowing freshening breezes to circulate while blocking out the summer sun. The rising hot air escapes through vents in the roof, replaced by the cooler outside air. This system of passive temperature control is effective enough to make artificial cooling unnecessary even during summer.

The house is oriented to take best advantage of solar gain from the winter sun, while additional heating is provided naturally via a geothermal heat pump. Heat transfer is minimised through energy-efficient environmentally-friendly insulation consisting of a mixture of wood fibre and recycled paper. Strategically positioned windows allow an abundance of natural light to flood the house.

Special attention was paid to the selection of materials and surface treatments in order to create a house that is healthy for the environment and its inhabitants. The external cladding consists of striking blueberry-tinted locally sourced recyclable timber. The main interior material is sustainably harvested spruce.

The combination of sustainable construction materials and a few simple passive design elements was all it took to optimise the energy efficiency and reduce the carbon footprint of this modern take on a traditional farmhouse.

1 Living
2 Dining
3 Kitchen
4 Bedroom
5 Library
6 Bathroom
7 Gallery

First floor

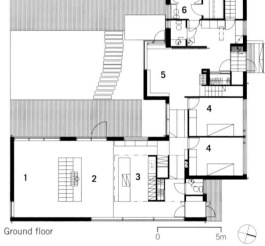

Ground floor

0   5m

Hover House 3

Venice, California, USA

Glen Irani Architects

Photography: Derek Rath Photography

The reasoning behind this reduction of built space is to reduce the amount of materials and energy consumed.

Situated on the Venice Canals, this house is the third in the architect's Hover House series of projects, which maximise living on small lots by suspending the building envelope above the lot in order to create a space for outdoor living environments. Conversely, interior living space is reduced in favour of less resource-intensive outdoor living amenities.

According to the architect, this three-bedroom, two-office home has 25 per cent less indoor floor space than an equivalent home. The reasoning behind this reduction of built space is to reduce the amount of materials and energy consumed in both the construction and running of larger houses. With Southern California's temperate climate, it seems both logical and desirable to connect residential architecture with the external environment and encourage a culture of semi-outdoor living.

In addition to the smaller building size, embodied energy is minimised through the house's exposed concrete walls[1] and man-made exterior slate panels. Low-CO_2-emission materials include tar-free, cold-applied roofing and low-VOC finishes.

The house is heated via a radiant hydronic heating system, and windows are strategically placed to make use of natural light and maximise natural ventilation, eliminating the need for an active air conditioning system. Roof-mounted photovoltaic panels are designed to produce 80 per cent of the house's electricity requirements.

Hover House 3, with its simple, precise design attends to the residential requirements of functionality, comfort and warmth. Yet more than a house, it represents a bold experiment in cultural and lifestyle change, pointing the way to a new form of living that embraces the outdoors while at the same time reducing costs, resource and material use, and therefore our carbon footprint.

1   The environmental impact of concrete is, to say the least, a hotly debated topic, and yet it has practically the lowest level of embodied energy relative to most other common building materials (http://www.yourhome.gov.au/technical/fs52.html).

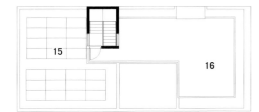

Roof level

Second floor

First floor

Garden level

0   3m

1 Garage
2 Outdoor kitchen
3 Outdoor living
4 Landscape
5 Bedroom
6 Laundry
7 Master closet
8 Master bathroom
9 Master bedroom
10 Office
11 Entry terrace
12 Kitchen
13 Media room
14 Dining
15 PV solar array
16 Roof terrace

Hover House 3 113

Kelly Residence

Los Angeles, California, USA

Abramson Teiger Architects

Photography: Richard Barnes
except rear elevation by David Lena

Sustainability features have been seamlessly integrated into the overall design, blending unobtrusively with the house's sleek modernist lines.

Kelly Residence is a very striking example of how sustainable design need not compromise style and architectural intent. Sustainability features have been seamlessly integrated into the overall design, blending unobtrusively with the house's sleek modernist lines.

The residence is articulated as 'boxes', each finished in white plaster and raised on steel pillars. Instead of being complete four-sided objects, one side of each 'box' has been replaced by high-density wood panels coated with phenolic resin. The panels, manufactured from sustainable products, act as a rain-screen and minimise thermal bridging. The skylights, which allow in an abundance of natural light, have a special coating which reduces heat/cooling loss. Floors are constructed of bamboo which, owing to its fast growth cycle, is perhaps one of the most sustainable building materials available.

The house has been divided into a private space above and public space below. At the lower level, large, expansive openings allow the garden to 'run' under the house. A reflecting pond positioned in front of a large glass wall is designed to provide evaporative cooling and air circulation. The top level of the house has a parents' side and a children's side, allowing each their privacy, with an 'umbilical cord' given form as a bridge between the two parts.

A zoned heating and air-conditioning system, including a high-efficiency unit in the master bedroom zone, minimises energy wastage in temperature control. Placed out of sight on the flat roof, photovoltaic cells supply the house with a renewable source of energy. All appliances used are energy-star rated, and the flash hot water system uses less energy than standard tank systems because the water is heated only on demand. Water consumption is minimised through the use of artificial lawn at the front of the house and a greywater reclamation drip irrigation system.

Kelly Residence shows just how far architects have come in discreetly incorporating sustainable design elements into the fabric of the architecture, illustrating how aesthetic and environmental concerns can coexist.

First floor

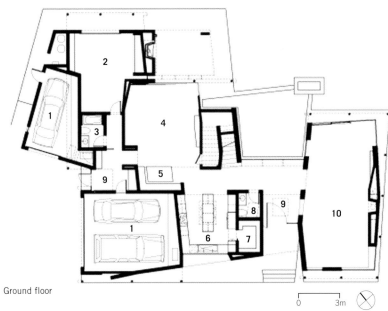

Ground floor

1	Garage	12	Bathroom
2	Guest bedroom	13	Closet
3	Guest bathroom	14	Storage
4	Family room	15	Laundry
5	Breakfast room	16	Mechanical room
6	Kitchen	17	Playroom
7	Pantry	18	Roof
8	Powder room	19	Master bedroom
9	Entry	20	Master closet
10	Living	21	Master bathroom
11	Bedroom		

0   3m

King Residence

Santa Monica, California, USA

John Friedman Alice Kimm Architects

Photography: Benny Chan/Fotoworks

Expansive glass sliding doors reduce the need for artificial lighting and enable ocean breezes to naturally ventilate the entire house.

The traditional typology of public front yard/ private backyard is inverted in the layout of King Residence, which instead opts for a structure whose living spaces and bedrooms open onto a relatively large garden and patio that face the public streets and surrounding houses in a design aimed at promoting a sense of neighbourliness and community.

The façade is composed primarily of plaster and cement board, a durable material that, unlike wood and vinyl, will not need to be replaced during the lifetime of the house and is recognised by the US Green Building Council's LEED certification program. The exterior's green and grey pattern is designed to echo the dappled light one sees when looking through a tree towards a sun-filled sky, visually integrating the house with its natural surroundings.

Echoing the openness of the house to the neighbourhood, the interior is a series of free-flowing, continuous spaces that foster a supportive, interactive family lifestyle. Generous use of skylights creates constantly changing light conditions that activate the interior. Expansive glass sliding doors reduce the need for artificial lighting and enable ocean breezes to naturally ventilate the entire house. A water feature on the east side of the house assists with natural evaporative cooling. Vertical wooden beams made of ipe shade the house from the sun, while strategically positioned deciduous trees provide a natural form of shading. These combined passive cooling elements are so effective the house does not require an active air conditioning system.

PV Ready

Choicedek

Eaves for Shading

Water Feature

Cement Board Siding

Radiant Heated flooring

Drought Resistant Landscaping

Passive Cooling

In-floor radiant heating provides an energy-efficient form of heating, and the roof is ready for the installation of a photovoltaic array, making this light, open house one striving to embrace both the community and the environment.

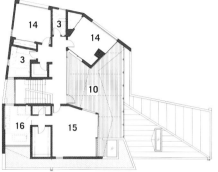

First floor

Ground floor

1 Office
2 Foyer
3 Bathroom
4 Wine cellar
5 Garage
6 Living
7 Laundry
8 Powder room
9 Kitchen
10 Patio
11 Fountain
12 Dining
13 Hang out room
14 Bedroom
15 Master bedroom
16 Master bathroom

0   6m

Kyneton House

Kyneton, Victoria, Australia

Marcus O'Reilly Architects

Photography: Dianna Snape

Natural light pours in through expansive north-facing windows, enlivening the active living, dining and kitchen areas.

Located on a leafy street in an historic part of the Victorian country town of Kyneton, clever design and use of light make this house seem larger than its modest 160 square metres (1722 square feet).

Much of this natural light pours in through expansive north-facing windows, enlivening the active living, dining and kitchen areas. The double-skillion roof, stretching east-to-west, opens up views to the garden and wooden deck outside, and also lets light into every room. Such is the abundance of daylight entering the house that, even on the greyest of days, artificial lighting is not required until night.

Carefully tapered wide eaves let in the warmth from the winter sun, which is absorbed by the thermal mass of the floor and southern walls. This, along with the insulation provided by the double-glazed windows and sealed air gap beneath the floor, provide such effective heat retention that, even given Kyneton's very cold winters, top-up heating is usually only required

for an hour or two in the morning. This is really quite impressive considering the average minimum temperatures can hover around 3 °C (37 °F) during winter.

This passive form of temperature control works just as effectively in summer, with the eaves preventing solar gain from the higher summer sun and the thermal mass keeping the house cool enough to not need an active air conditioning system.

Discreetly positioned grid-connected solar panels provide electricity to the house. Solar panels also supply household hot water needs and heat the water for the hydronic heating system which has heat panels integrated into both the floor and the polished concrete kitchen bench. Water requirements are supplemented by the rainwater harvested and stored in tastefully camouflaged water tanks near the front of the house.

Compact, light and unassuming, Kyneton House makes sustainability look easy.

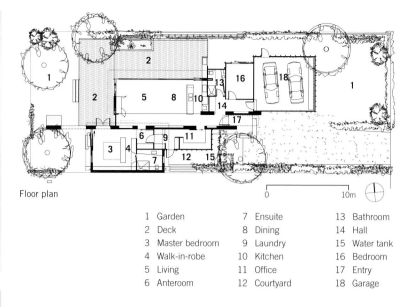

Floor plan

1	Garden	7	Ensuite	13	Bathroom
2	Deck	8	Dining	14	Hall
3	Master bedroom	9	Laundry	15	Water tank
4	Walk-in-robe	10	Kitchen	16	Bedroom
5	Living	11	Office	17	Entry
6	Anteroom	12	Courtyard	18	Garage

La Casa Verde

San Francisco, California, USA

Architecture: John Lum Architecture

Landscape: Arterra Landscape Architects

Photography: Richard Barnes and Sharon Risedorph (exterior)

Electricity is generated from renewable energy
sources via a photovoltaic array and wind turbine.

Designed to be completely self-sustaining, La Casa Verde was one of the first homes to participate in the LEED Pilot Homes Program, with the goal of achieving zero net energy use through a blend of cutting-edge technology and passive design features.

Electricity is generated from renewable energy sources via a photovoltaic array and wind turbine, while the consumption of power is optimised by a smart computer system that operates and monitors lighting, heating, cooling and ventilation. Water is recycled through a greywater irrigation system that utilises rainwater captured from roofs and patios before being stored in underground cisterns in the backyard.

Natural light floods the house through clerestory windows that top the three-storey glass stairwell. The combination of operable windows throughout the house, a whole house fan and an atrium chimney facilitate natural ventilation and passive cooling. The design takes advantage of the warm weather in the Mission District area of San Francisco by opening up the house to extensive landscaped areas and roof terraces featuring native plants watered by the rainwater catchment system. A solar thermal system heats the indoor pool, which is filtered without the use of chemicals.

An equal amount of thought was given to the environmental impact of the materials used in the construction of the house. Fencing and framework salvaged from the original structure on the site were reused to minimise landfill. More innovative use of recycled material is displayed in the stair railings created from local scrap steel pipe. Wherever possible, materials with at least some element of sustainability were used in the construction. Resin panels are sandwiched with recycled materials, the majority of the concrete used has fly-ash content, concrete counters are coloured with embedded particles of recycled rice hulls, and FSC-certified Santa Maria Tropical wood was used for floors and ceilings.

Colourful, open and highly original, La Casa Verde is an innovative celebration of the possibilities of sustainable design.

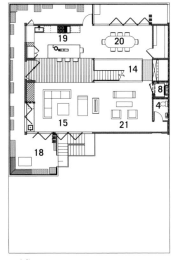

Second floor

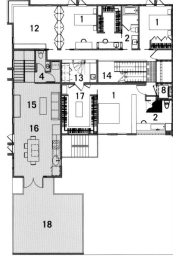

First floor

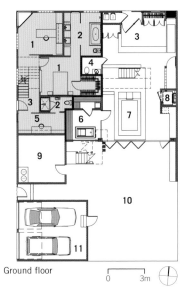

Ground floor

0   3m

1 Bedroom
2 Bathroom
3 Entry
4 Powder room
5 Office
6 Steam room/
   Sauna
7 Pool and bar
8 Elevator
9 Mechanical
   room
10 Rear yard
11 Garage
12 Craft room
13 Laundry
14 Atrium
15 Living
16 Kitchen/
   Casual dining
17 Closet
18 Outdoor deck
19 Kitchen
20 Dining
21 Media room

Loch Derg

Nenagh, County Tipperary, Ireland

Box Architecture (Ashlene Ross and Gary Mongey)

Photography: Paul Tierney Photography

Embodied energy levels were conserved and material waste minimised by preserving the fabric of the original cottage.

The Loch Derg project breathed new life into a dilapidated and little-used circa-1940s cottage in the Irish country town of Nenagh. Rather than completely demolish the existing structure, embodied energy levels were conserved and material waste minimised by preserving the fabric of the original cottage as much as possible. The existing rear extension was pulled down and three new elements added—a living block, glazed link and shed.

The new living block is a simple linear form, tucked behind the existing cottage while affording a view of the loch and flood plain to the north. It contains an open-plan living, kitchen and dining area, while the sleeping accommodation is housed within the original cottage. Large glazed joinery elements and an extensive wall-to-wall roof light allow penetration and movement of natural light within the living block, while light is drawn into the original cottage via folding glazed doors and more roof lights. The existing windows to the front of the cottage were retained and preserved.

All walls were dry-lined to improve insulation, and the southwest-facing glazed joinery harnesses warmth from the winter sun and provides an abundance of natural light. A low carbon-emission wood pellet boiler and wood pellet stove are a sufficient heat source, while solar panels mounted on the southwest face of the pitched roof assist water heating. High-performance glazing helps retain internal heat and generally contributes to the energy efficiency of the building. A wide sliding door covers almost the entire southeast-facing side of the new living volume, opening up to the external courtyard and allowing for natural ventilation.

Alongside modern forms and materials, the design of Loch Derg introduces some very simple passive solar design strategies while maintaining an aesthetic connection with its rural setting.

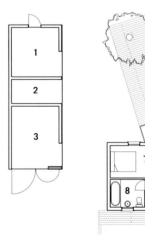

1 Stable
2 Wash room
3 Storeroom
4 Living
5 Kitchen/Dining
6 Glazed link
7 Bedroom
8 Bathroom
9 Entry hall
10 Dressing room

Marcus Beach House

Marcus Beach, Queensland, Australia

Bark Design Architects

Photography: Christopher Frederick Jones

This is a house that quite literally opens itself up to the outdoors.

A change of ownership was the impetus for alterations and additions in 2009 that refined and explored new design concepts for this coastal Queensland beach house originally designed by Bark in 2002. That the house has been constructed around a courtyard containing a 50-year-old Moreton Bay ash, which acts as a centrepiece to the two pavilions and which almost every room in the house connects with, is indicative of the respect the design shows its natural surroundings and how indoors and outdoors have been integrated.

This is a house that quite literally opens itself up to the outdoors, allowing in an abundance of daylight and freshening breezes for natural ventilation through operable glass walls and windows. The indoor living/dining area extends out into a generous double-height decked outdoor space protected from the sun while cooled by the easterly breezes blowing in from the Pacific Ocean. Translucent polycarbonate cladding allows light to enter while reflecting heat and providing insulation.

High-level operable windows capture daylight and allow heat to escape in an effective stack-effect natural cooling system that overrides the need for an active air conditioning system. This system of passive cooling is assisted by the internal stairwell and high-level louvres enabling warm air to escape. Timber shades on the east façade provide a defence against the heat of the morning sun, while elsewhere generous overhangs shade the house from direct sunlight. The landscape is protected by a perimeter wall wrapped in endemic vines, providing an acoustic 'green' buffer to a busy road to the west.

Careful attention was paid to the minimisation of wastage during construction, with some material reclaimed from the original structure used for the alterations and additions. Timber used for screening, outdoor seating and the internal structure was sourced locally, helping minimise embodied energy.

There is a lightness and a breeziness about this house that, combined with its sense of sophistication and respect for its environment, makes it more than just a typical beach house.

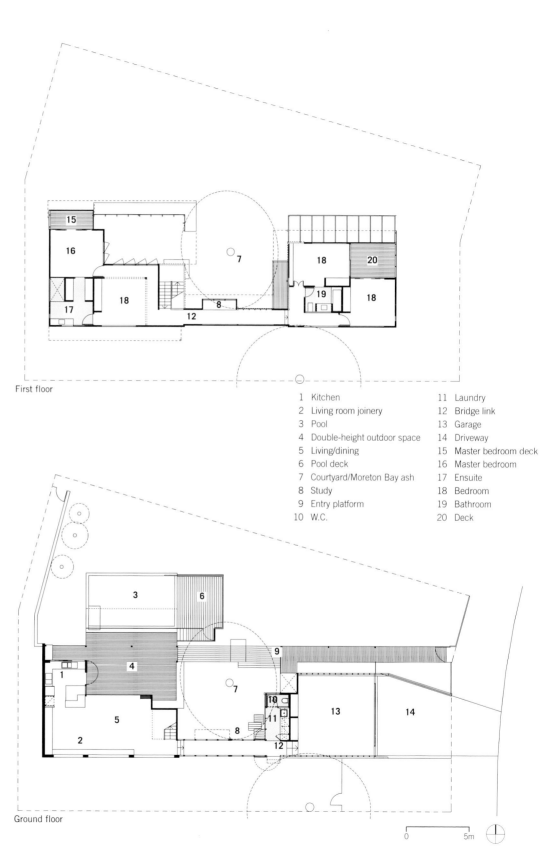

First floor

1 Kitchen
2 Living room joinery
3 Pool
4 Double-height outdoor space
5 Living/dining
6 Pool deck
7 Courtyard/Moreton Bay ash
8 Study
9 Entry platform
10 W.C.

11 Laundry
12 Bridge link
13 Garage
14 Driveway
15 Master bedroom deck
16 Master bedroom
17 Ensuite
18 Bedroom
19 Bathroom
20 Deck

Ground floor

0   5m

Marcus Beach House   137

Margarido House

Oakland, California, USA

Onion Flats, Plumbob, Medium Plenty

Photography: Mariko Reed

Some measure of energy efficiency and sustainability seems to exist in every element of the house's design.

Sustainability in design, construction and operation was a fundamental concern from the very early planning stages of the Margarido House, which was part of the LEED for Homes pilot program and eventually achieved LEED for Homes Platinum certification, being 55 per cent more energy efficient than required by California's Title 24 energy standards.

This is hardly surprising, considering some measure of energy efficiency and sustainability seems to exist in every element of the house's design, from the solar hot water and radiant floor heating system to the use of VOC-free paint and other environmentally-friendly materials and finishes, all sourced locally wherever possible. All concrete used in the house has a minimum 25 per cent fly ash content (a by-product of the coal industry that often ends up as landfill), and benchtops and some outdoor furniture are made of recycled concrete sourced from local suppliers.

Initially anticipated to provide only 50 per cent of household electricity requirements, the photovoltaic array exceeded expectations in supplying 120 per cent. This exceptional performance is no doubt in part a result of the house's highly efficient insulation. Partly built into the slope of the hill, the house is able to make use of natural geothermal temperature control. Add to this a soy-based spray-foam insulation in the walls and the thermally broken aluminium frames for the double-glazed low-E coated windows, and you have a house that practically eliminates energy wastage in heating and cooling.

The intensive green roof (which means it is strong enough to be walked on and enjoyed as a functional garden) consists of specially selected drought-tolerant plants and provides the house with a further layer of insulation as well as managing rainwater run-off. Groundwater, captured via the permeable paving, and rainwater is stored in 15,000-litre underground cisterns and used for irrigation.

Margarido House has become something of a paragon of sustainability, with hundreds of designers, architects, builders and homeowners having toured the home to learn about and be inspired by the possibilities of sustainable design.

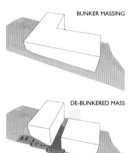

BUNKER MASSING	CARVE & FRAGMENT	TERRAIN SHAPING
DE-BUNKERED MASS	KNUCKLE	DETAILED MASSING

Massing

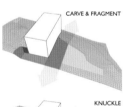

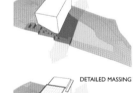

Section A looking north

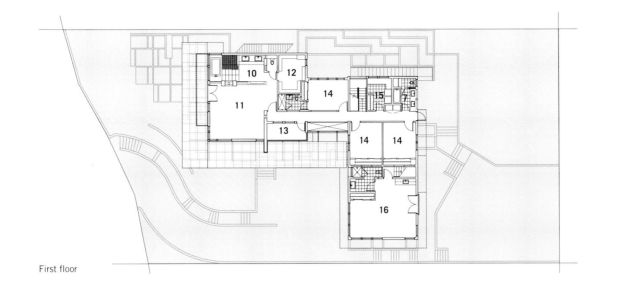

First floor

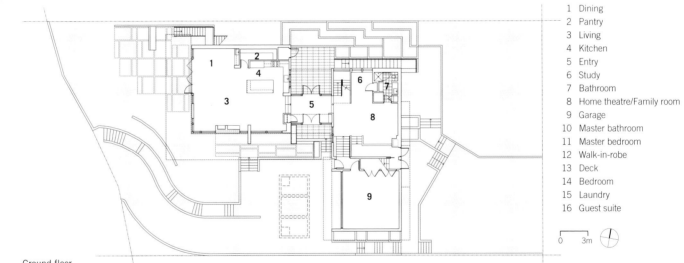

Ground floor

1 Dining
2 Pantry
3 Living
4 Kitchen
5 Entry
6 Study
7 Bathroom
8 Home theatre/Family room
9 Garage
10 Master bathroom
11 Master bedroom
12 Walk-in-robe
13 Deck
14 Bedroom
15 Laundry
16 Guest suite

0   3m

Margarido House   141

Mt. Veeder Residence

Napa, California, USA

Arkin Tilt Architects

Photography: Edward Caldwell Photography

Simple passive solar strategies are combined with a sophisticated heating system.

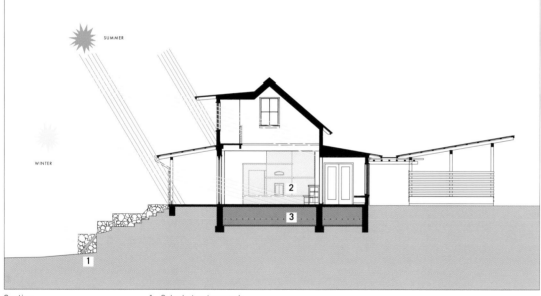

Section

1 Solar hot water panels
2 Masonry heater
3 Solar hot water heated
   sand bed

This passive solar farmhouse is situated on a 25-acre organic family vineyard and winery known as Camalie Vineyards, and serves as the family residence and home office.

Simple passive solar strategies such as careful orientation, porches and overhangs, thermal mass and stack ventilation are combined with a sophisticated heating system that integrates hot water provided by solar collectors along with a heat transfer coil within the masonry heater. The primary heat sink is a solar-heated deep sand bed system that keeps the main floor at a constant temperature, supplemented with hydronic radiant heating in the bedroom wing (pre-heated by solar and wood, with back-up from a highly efficient heat pump).

Operable windows provide fresh air, and thermostatically-controlled whole house fans provide night flush cooling during the warmer summer and fall months. A recirculation duct and fans move cool air from the lowest level up to the loft in summer, then reverses the flow

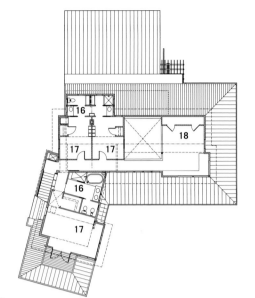

First floor

1 Powder room
2 Mechanical room
3 Media room
4 Carport
5 Laundry/Mudroom
6 Pantry
7 Entry
8 Office
9 Living
10 Dining
11 Kitchen
12 Guest bathroom
13 Guest bedroom
14 Screen porch
15 Solar hot water panels
16 Bathroom
17 Bedroom
18 Sitting room

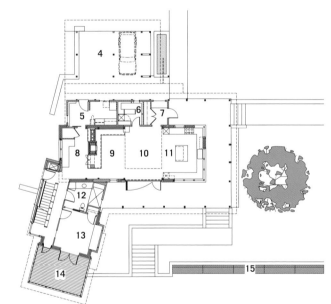

Ground floor

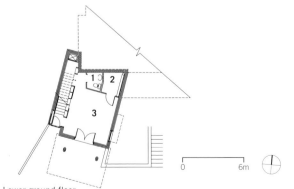

Lower ground floor

0   6m

bringing warm air to the media room during winter months.

The wood-framed walls on the upper levels of the house are insulated with full-cavity, wet-sprayed cellulose insulation made from recycled newspaper. Windows are primarily aluminum-clad with high-performance glazing.

The house is protected from the summer afternoon sun by the hillside to the west while remaining open to the surrounding vineyard, and has been carefully positioned so that natural light reaches at least two sides of every room. In some cases transom windows (above interior doors) or interior windows are utilised to both help spaces feel larger and provide daylight. The children's bedrooms feature lofts above the hallway with windows that allow the low winter sun to heat these rooms. Throughout the project south- and east-facing windows ensure solar gain, with bays and roof overhangs providing solar control to prevent overheating during the summer and early autumn months. On a typical day the owners do not turn on any interior lights.

Oppenheimer Residence

Sag Harbor, New York, USA

Pablo Jendretzki

Photography: Alejandro Wirth

The house is equipped with an energy efficient HVAC system, and solar roof panels contribute a portion of the house's energy requirements.

The concept behind this redesign of an existing house in the Sag Harbor area of New York was to connect the exterior with the interior spaces, making more of a feature of the surrounding woodland. Apart from a couple of fixed windows, the original house was almost completely closed off from the outside. The installation of strategically positioned and generously proportioned windows and glass sliding doors allows natural light to flood in and open up the house to the landscape. Cross ventilation via the sliding doors at the east and west of the house allow for natural circulation during warmer months.

Though not LEED certified, sustainability considerations were an important part of the design. In addition to the recycled cedar exterior, interior counter and vanity tops are made of reconstituted stone, and cork was used for the underlay of the lower-level flooring. Cork not only provides effective thermal insulation but is a highly sustainable material. It comes from the bark of the cork oak (*Quercus suber*), harvested

roughly every nine years from a mature tree, so doesn't actually require the cutting down of a single tree. If harvested properly, the bark regenerates without any negative impact. Cork could in fact be described as the quintessential sustainable material.

The house is equipped with an energy-efficient HVAC system, and solar roof panels contribute a portion of the house's energy requirements. Water consumption is reduced through the harvesting of rainfall for use as greywater.

With an exterior constructed of recycled cedar, there is a lightness about the house that sees it blend unobtrusively with its surrounds. Constructed on a limited budget, the Oppenheimer Residence shows that some simple design elements and a careful and intelligent choice of materials can go some way towards producing a house that, if not quite there, is certainly on the right path towards sustainability.

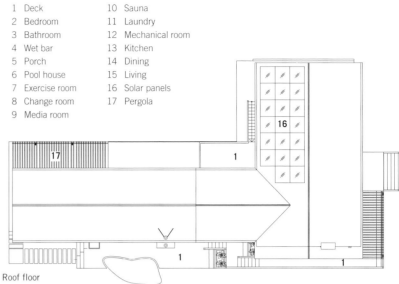

1 Deck
2 Bedroom
3 Bathroom
4 Wet bar
5 Porch
6 Pool house
7 Exercise room
8 Change room
9 Media room
10 Sauna
11 Laundry
12 Mechanical room
13 Kitchen
14 Dining
15 Living
16 Solar panels
17 Pergola

Roof floor

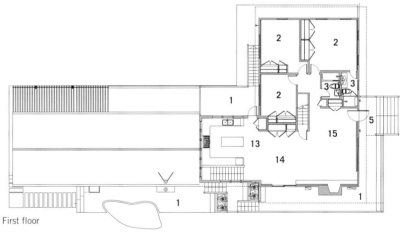

First floor

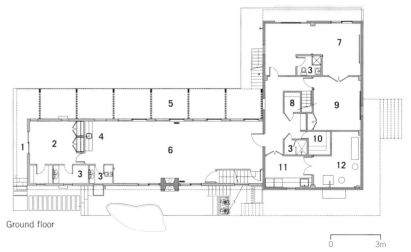

Ground floor

0   3m

Oppenheimer Residence   149

Palmyra House

Nandgaon, Maharashtra, India

Studio Mumbai

Photography: Helene Binet, Studio Mumbai, Prabuddha Dasgupta

Its wooden structure appears to have risen from the ground, so unobtrusively is it nestled among the surrounding palm trees.

Palmyra House isn't just gentle on the environment, it treats it with a kind of reverence, so lightly does it impinge on its surroundings, its very positioning resulting from the desire to preserve as many trees as possible on its site, a 1-acre functioning coconut plantation. A holiday retreat located in an agricultural region 45 kilometres southeast of Mumbai, its wooden structure appears to have risen from the ground, so unobtrusively is it nestled among the surrounding palm trees.

And in a way, it *has* risen from the ground, with a frame constructed of sustainable, locally harvested *ain* wood, assembled using traditional interlocking joinery. The entire house was in fact built by local labourers using handcrafted materials and traditional building techniques. Operable teak wood louvres and fixed louvres made of locally sourced, sustainable palmyra literally open the house up, allowing in natural light and making use of the freshening ocean

breeze and overhead palms for ventilation and to help dissipate the heat. The foundation stone and the sand used for the plaster were also sourced locally.

Though not native to India, the palmyra species of palm tree is widely cultivated there and is considered one of the country's most valuable and versatile trees, prized for its manifold uses, with almost every part of the tree being of some utility. The leaves can be used for thatching and making such things as baskets and fans, the fruit can of course be eaten, and the trunk makes a strong building material. Best suited to the drier parts of India, in ideal conditions it can grow to a height of 30 metres, though its average height is around 12 to 18 metres.

Palmyra House is certainly a fitting tribute to this most versatile of trees. Warm and earthy and yet undeniably modern, it is a wonderful blend of style and sustainability.

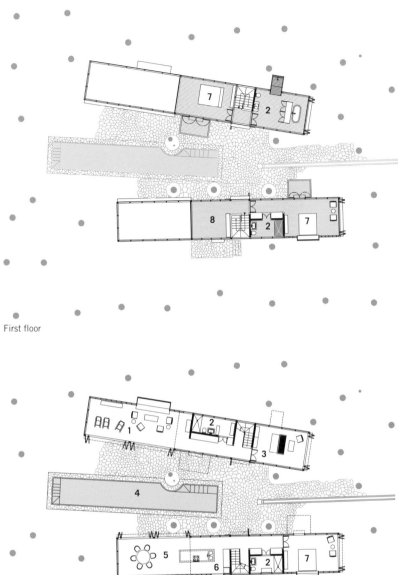

First floor

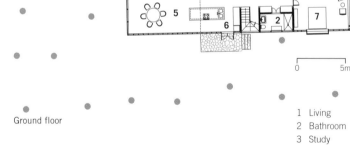

Ground floor

1 Living
2 Bathroom
3 Study
4 Pool
5 Dining
6 Kitchen
7 Bedroom
8 Sitting room

0   5m

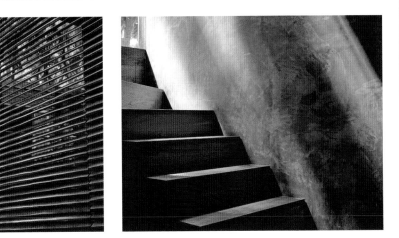

Pepper Drive House

Los Altos, California, USA

Mark English Architects

Photography: Norma Lopez Molina

The Pepper Drive house, with its emphasis on energy efficiency and verified quality of construction, exceeds California's strict energy code by 30 per cent.

The sustainability of the Pepper Drive house is measured according to the GreenPoint Rating system, an alternative to the LEED system developed by BuildItGreen, a consortium of building professionals in California. The GreenPoint checklist is wide-ranging, including sustainable features relating to insulation, finishes, plumbing, use of renewable energy, flooring, water conservation, and appliances and lighting, among other things. Each option on the checklist is assigned a certain number of points, and the resulting total is the project's GreenPoint score. The combined total of all options exceeds 300 GreenPoints, though no one project is expected to achieve a perfect score. The intention of the program is to provide a wide array of options from which to choose, to encourage people to choose green building alternatives wherever possible.

Along with all these optional measures, the GreenPoint Rating system includes a few mandatory ones, including 50 per cent construction waste diversion and a 15 per cent margin over California's energy code performance minimum (Title 24). The California energy code has strict requirements relating to allowable levels of heat transmission (U-value) and solar heat gain. The Pepper Drive house, with its emphasis on energy efficiency and verified quality of construction, achieved a GreenPoint score of 113 and exceeds California's strict energy code by 30 per cent. This has to some extent been achieved through high-performance windows, a high-efficiency furnace and water heater, radiant heat barrier and low-leakage duct system. Further energy savings are made through the additional thermal mass of the 5/8 drywall, solar shading provided by overhangs, low-emitting insulation products and low-water landscaping.

On a more aesthetic level, the stylish, stately interior contains a dramatic two-storey staircase acting as a centrepiece, while the material palette of the exterior is natural, consisting of an integrally coloured cement plaster that lends this exquisite, environmentally-friendly house a certain understated appearance.

First floor

Ground floor

0   3m

1 Foyer
2 Closet
3 Office
4 Bathroom
5 Area open to above
6 Bedroom
7 Living
8 Garage
9 Hall
10 Mudroom/Laundry
11 Utility room
12 Wet bar
13 Pantry
14 Kitchen
15 Family room
16 Outdoor patio
17 Area open to below
18 Dressing room
19 Master bedroom
20 Master bathroom
21 Terrace

Rainbow House

Santa Monica, California, USA

Minarc

Photography: Nancy Pastor, David Lena,
Erla Dögg Ingjaldsdóttir, Vladan

Iron from the original staircase was salvaged, and wood reclaimed from the original structure has been used as beams in the courtyard atrium.

The reuse and recycling of materials has been maximised in this conversion of a five-unit apartment building into a single-family residence, stemming from the architects' commitment to responsible, sustainable design and their intrinsic dislike of waste. More than 50 per cent of the original structure has been kept, and to minimise embodied energy and avoid the use of unnecessary chemicals, no paint, carpet or tiles were used in the construction. Materials and fixtures that weren't reused, such as garage doors and sinks, were donated to Habitat for Humanity, an organisation that builds homes for the needy. Iron from the original staircase was salvaged, and wood reclaimed from the original structure has been used as beams in the courtyard atrium.

Kitchen cabinets and chairs are made from material manufactured from recycled rubber and cork, and the kitchen countertops and dining-room table are made from recycled wood scraps. The bathroom sinks (RUBBiSH® recycled rubber sinks) are made from the rubber of old car tyres through an ingenious process that won Minarc an *Architect* magazine 2010 R+D award.

Intelligent use of generously proportioned sliding windows and doors in the master bedroom and ground floor provides cross-circulation and plenty of natural daylight, also dissolving the barriers between outdoors and indoors. This is best captured in the living area that opens up onto an outdoor veranda/dining area while bringing freshening breezes into the house. Solar gain can be controlled through the manipulation of solar rays, or sun shades, fixed to some of the windows, helping regulate internal temperature. These passive elements are so effective no air conditioning system is required.

Further energy savings are made via the solar thermal water heating system and the solar thermal radiant flooring that heats the house when required.

Rainbow House derives its name from the light refracted through the glass railings, which bathes the house in the colours of the rainbow; and this seems to encapsulate the sense of optimism the architects had in designing the house, seeing the possibilities rather than restrictions of sustainable design.

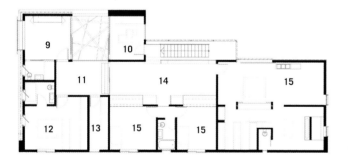

First floor

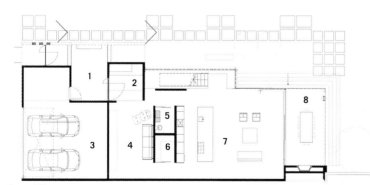

Ground floor

1 Entry courtyard
2 Entry
3 Garage
4 TV room
5 Powder room
6 Pantry
7 Kitchen and living
8 Dining veranda
9 Gym
10 Office
11 Courtyard
12 Guest room
13 Laundry
14 Family room
15 Bedroom

Ross Street House

Madison, Wisconsin, USA

Richard Wittschiebe Hand

Photography: Zane Williams

The house used almost 50 per cent less energy than expected in its first year, the result of a mix of passive and active features.

Considerable investigation, thought and research was put into the sustainability strategy underpinning the design and construction of the Ross Street house, ultimately leading to it achieving LEED for Homes Platinum certification.

Significantly smaller than the average size of a newly-built house in the US at just 158 square metres (1700 square feet), it was originally allocated a HERS (Home Energy Rating System) rating of 42, meaning it was predicted to use around 58 per cent less energy than the HERS reference home (based on the 2006 International Energy Conservation Code). The house exceeded even this impressive estimate by using almost 50 per cent less energy than expected in its first year, the result of a mix of passive and active features.

Photovoltaic panels located on the detached garage generate more than half the annual household electricity demand, with energy star appliances used throughout the house to optimise usage.

The primary building form is a simple two-storey 'light box' volume facing due south, with the overhang and fixed exterior brise-soleil positioned to capture as much of the winter sun as possible while providing shading in summer. There is limited east–west fenestration; however, west-facing portholes activate the interior with beams of light. East-facing ribbon windows provide morning light in the dining area and bedrooms.

Water is conserved via a landscape comprised of native perennials with no turf grass. All rainwater

falling on the site is either collected in cisterns or directed via bioswales to a rain garden.

Sustainability was also a consideration in the more minor touches to the house, such as through the use of low-VOC paints and sealants, the installation of locally-sourced hardwood flooring, and the ground floor polished concrete flooring, reducing the use of finishing materials.

Awarded the 2010 Future Landmark Award for Innovative New Design from the Madison Trust for Historic Preservation, this modern home is both sensitive to the environment and respectful of its surroundings.

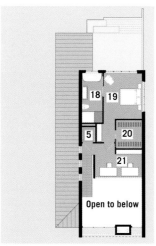

First floor

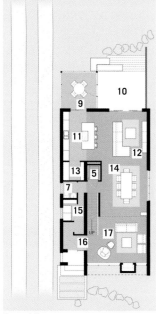

Ground floor

Lower floor

1 Beer making room
2 Bathroom
3 Bedroom
4 Mechanical room
5 Future elevator
6 Workroom
7 Larder (cold cellar)
8 Rumpus room
9 Screen porch
10 Deck
11 Kitchen
12 Den
13 Pantry
14 Dining
15 Laundry
16 Foyer
17 Living
18 Master bathroom
19 Master bedroom
20 Walk-in-robe
21 Study

0   6m

Schierle House

Gerzen, Germany

Matthias Benz Architecture & Design

Photography: Rathschek Schiefer and Thomas Benz

Energy-efficient elements and the use of recycled
materials were integral to the house's construction.

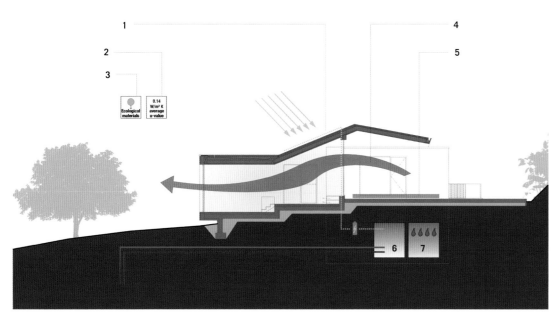

1. Ecological materials

0.14 W/m² K average u-value

1 Roof ready for photovoltaic
panels to support heat pump
2 Minimal energy consumption
(marginal heat loss through
external walls—low U-value)
3 Use of ecological-friendly
materials (timber with cellulose
insulation …)
4 Natural ventilation
5 Concrete flooring as thermal
mass
6 Heat pump with depth probe
7 Rainwater collection

Built on land formerly occupied by a farmhouse,
the design of Schierle House had to first
overcome a number of environmental challenges
unrelated to sustainability. Located in Gerzen,
a picture-postcard town in the Bavarian region
of Germany, strict urban regulations required
the house to have a pitched roof. It was also
important that the house not obstruct any
neighbouring residences' panoramic view of the
valley below. The resulting design is one that
both respects the tradition of the surrounding
architecture and yet displays a contemporary
individuality.

Sustainability was also an important
consideration, with energy-efficient elements
and the use of recycled materials integral to the
house's construction. The pitched roof, made
of slate, ended up being a visually spectacular
feature of the house, creating the perfect blend
of modernism and environmental integration.

Effective insulation is achieved through the use
of flax, cellulose and wood fibre board, all low

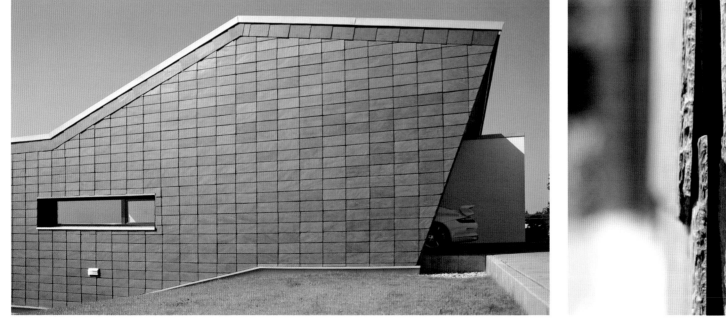

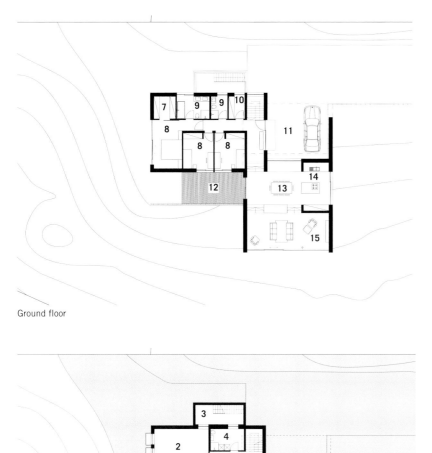

Ground floor

Basement

1 Hobby room/Gym
2 Storage room/Studio
3 Courtyard
4 Laundry
5 Plant room
6 Larder
7 Dressing room
8 Bedroom
9 Bathroom
10 Wardrobe
11 Carport
12 Terrace
13 Dining
14 Kitchen
15 Living

0   3m

thermal conductivity materials that minimise the loss of heat. The house is heated geothermally, via five 35-metre-deep geothermal probes, and large south-facing windows ensure maximum natural lighting. During the summer, the 4-metre vertical slope of the house uses the upward blowing breeze to help cool the interiors.

Schierle House's total energy consumption is 65 per cent less than that allowed by the German energy saving ordinance/regulation (ENeV). The house has in fact become something of a model of energy efficiency, being part of a 'sustainable architecture' tour organised by Bavaria's Chamber of Architecture in 2009. The planned addition of photovoltaic panels and a rainwater collection system will only further improve the house's energy efficiency and sustainability credentials.

Shelter House

Yport, Normandy, France

Franklin Azzi Architecture

Photography: Franklin Azzi Architecture,
Emmanuelle Blanc

The house is not connected to the grid, being self-sufficient in terms of water and power.

This holiday home with sumptuous views of the English Channel and overlooking the beautiful small French coastal town of Yport is a reconstruction and extension of a tiny (18 square metres, or 194 square feet) rundown cottage formerly used as a hunters' shelter. The original brick structure was retained and restored, while timber was used for the additions partly because its lighter weight made it easier to transport to this difficult-to-access site. Much of the timber extension was constructed in the workshop and then transported to the site in sections. All building materials used in the project were sourced within 100 kilometres (62 miles) of the site.

Severe zoning regulations strictly limited the size of the expansion, so the two timber deck wings at the side of the house are designed to be enclosed by canvas tents, providing comfortable temporary living quarters while not breaching the zoning laws.

A thin concrete slab with radiant heating and ipe wood decking forms the additional flooring to the left and right of the house. The house is not connected to the grid, being self-sufficient in terms of water and power. Power and hot water are supplied through a mix of solar and geothermal energy, while water is drawn from a bore drilled into an aquifer on site. The house is equipped with a rainwater recovery system and a triple filtering system that separates fresh drinking water, greywater for washing and toilet flushing, and blackwater to be stored in the septic tank. The design of the house also makes wonderful use of natural light and ventilation.

The style of this idyllic cottage house is beautifully in keeping with its surroundings, and its environmental impact has been minimised through its responsible and creative use of existing materials, its restrained size and its energy self-sufficiency.

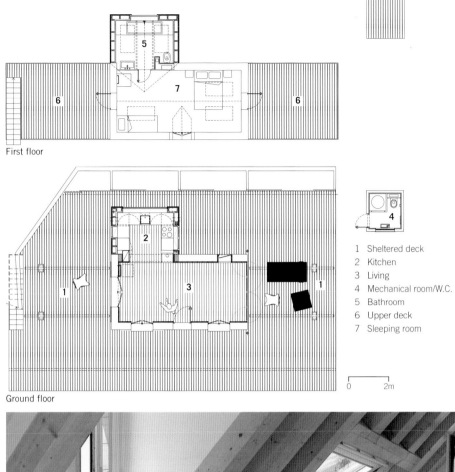

First floor

Ground floor

0   2m

1   Sheltered deck
2   Kitchen
3   Living
4   Mechanical room/W.C.
5   Bathroom
6   Upper deck
7   Sleeping room

Shelter House   173

Skyline Residence

Los Angeles, California, USA

Belzberg Architects

Photography: Benny Chan, Fotoworks

Protection from direct sunlight and maximum daylighting informed the organisation of spaces and the composition of exterior wall treatments.

The design of Skyline Residence makes pragmatic use of the challenges presented by its site on a ridgeline in the Hollywood Hills, with some of the measures aimed at causing the least environmental disturbance also turning out to be the most cost effective.

The severity of the slope and the dense granite stone beneath the surface meant minimal excavation was carried out. This reduced the amount of expendable energy in operating machinery and involved only removing earth that could be reused in other areas of the project. The excavated granite, for example, was decomposed and re-used to level drain pipes, under concrete slabs, as a drainage field under the pool and as a walking surface for the viewing deck above the garage. Wood framing and wood flooring leftovers acquired from a nearby construction site were made use of, while the low-E glazing, steel, CMU blocks and indigenous aggregates (crushed rock, sand, gravel) were all locally sourced.

The positioning of the house takes advantage of natural elements. Protection from direct sunlight and maximum daylighting informed the organisation of spaces and the composition of exterior wall treatments. The southwest-facing façade is shaded from the heat of the sun by a custom screen made of a low-formaldehyde-emitting composite lumber, while the northeast-facing glass walls open up external views and provide every room in the house with natural light.

Oversized, hinged double-doors open on either side of the living room, inviting the prevailing winds to flow uninterrupted through the interior space. The corridor leading to the bedrooms has openings at either ends which facilitate an airflow past each room, and openings from each room to the rear yard draw on the cool air moving down the corridor through the length of the house.

Through an understanding of the site conditions and local climate patterns, the very sophisticated

Skyline Residence has made use of some very simple design elements to minimise its impact on the environment.

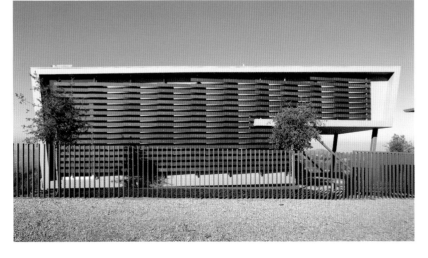

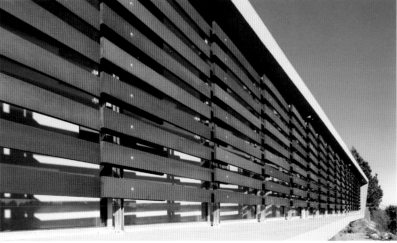

1 Guest house and carport
   (two levels)
2 Turn-around driveway and
   outdoor movie seating
3 Outdoor movie deck
   (garage below)
4 Living and dining area
5 Pool
6 Kitchen
7 Bedroom
8 Master bathroom
9 Master bedroom

Skyline Dr.

Site plan

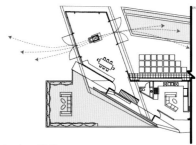

Natural ventilation

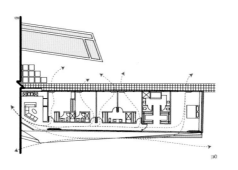

Solar Active House

Regensburg, Germany

fabi architekten bda

Photography: Herbert Stolz

The technological sophistication that enables the Solar Active house to achieve its impressive level of energy efficiency is seamlessly woven into the fabric of its architecture.

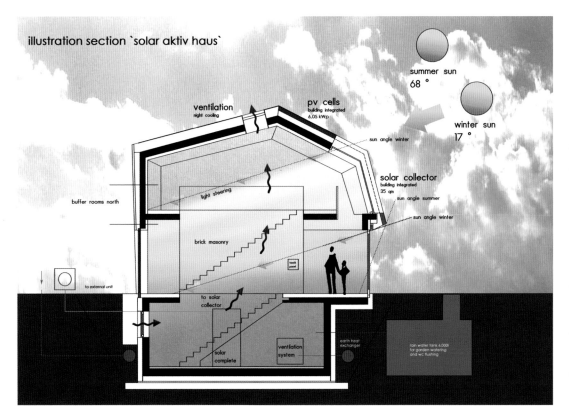

illustration section `solar aktiv haus`

summer sun
68 °

winter sun
17 °

ventilation
night cooling

pv cells
building integrated
6,05 kWp

sun angle winter

solar collector
building integrated
35 qm
sun angle summer

sun angle winter

light steering

buffer rooms north

brick masonry

to external unit

to solar collector

solar complete

ventilation system

earth heat exchanger

rain water tank 6,000l
for garden watering
and wc flushing

This prototype solar active house commissioned by the solar technology company Sonnenkraft envisions the kind of solar energy optimisation measures that will be standard in residential buildings by 2020, looking beyond energy *savings* made through passive design elements to the active *production* of solar energy. First and foremost, however, the house is designed to be lived in, and though the technology is critical, it does not override the importance of the house's liveability, and the comfort and needs of those living in the house remain the primary focus.

The orientation and crystal-like shape of the house take advantage of the trajectory of the sun for optimal solar winter gain and harnessing of solar energy via 55 square metres (592 square feet) of photovoltaic panels and 35 square metres (377 square feet) of solar thermal panels. The diamond-shaped panels alternate at sharp angles with bonded fibre cement tiles, and the anthracite-coloured cladding sheets ensure the panels blend unobtrusively with the exterior of the house. Based on energy consumption levels

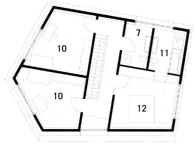

First floor

determined via thorough calculations and simulations performed by the Frauenhofer Institute for Solar Energy Systems, the house generates all its thermal energy needs and a surplus of electricity.

A compact automated smart system regulates the passive use of solar energy from the south and west in winter and automatically shades the southern surface of the glass during the summer, while mechanical cross-ventilation and the natural ventilation from the lower level up to the roof ensures optimal air exchange. Through a connection with a weather station, the system measures temperature, CO_2 and humidity to maintain interior comfort levels.

The technological sophistication that enables the Solar Active house to achieve its impressive level of energy efficiency is seamlessly woven into the fabric of its architecture, resulting in a low-maintenance sustainable house that is comfortable, adaptable and a tranquil retreat from the pressures of modern life.

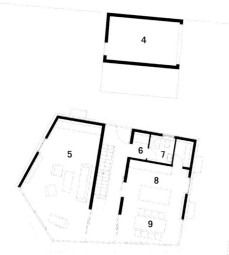

Ground floor

1 Storeroom
2 Mechanical room
3 Laundry
4 Garage
5 Living
6 Wardrobe
7 Bathroom
8 Kitchen
9 Dining
10 Bedroom
11 Master bathroom
12 Master bedroom

Basement floor

0   5m

Steigereiland 2.0

Steigereiland, The Netherlands

FARO Architecten

Photography: John Lewis Marshall

The house's entire electricity and hot water needs are provided by twin wind turbines located on the roof and a photovoltaic array.

The carbon-neutral Steigereiland 2.0 was designed and constructed in accordance with the 'cradle-to-cradle' (C2C) principle, which in part proposes that all synthetic materials used in the construction process be non-harmful and non-toxic and able to be used over and over again in their intended or original form rather than 'downcycled' into a lower-grade product. Non-synthetic, or organic, materials used must be able to be disposed of without causing any environmental harm or damage, or even have some sort of ecological benefit.

Steigereiland 2.0's incredible energy efficiency is the result of a combination of a range of simple and more sophisticated technology that includes triple-glazed windows with insulated framing, cellulose roof insulation, adobe walls containing PCMs (Phase Changing Materials), 100 per cent liquid-tight joints, and heat recovery ventilation. In line with the C2C principle, all insulation materials used are organic.

A ground source heat exchanger two metres beneath the house provides cooling in summer and heating in winter. Water heated in vacuum tube collectors discretely located in the roof cornice of the house is used for the radiant floor heating. Windows are positioned to provide natural light and solar gain in winter while being protected from the summer sun.

The house's entire electricity and hot water needs are provided by twin wind turbines located on the roof and a photovoltaic array, with any excess capacity directed back into the grid.

The living area of the house rests atop a horizontally-positioned tree trunk salvaged from an Amsterdam canal during the restoration of a quay. The exterior façade consists of burnt wood. This traditional Japanese technique preserves the wood naturally, eliminating the need for paint or impregnation.

The warmth and homeliness of Steigereiland 2.0 belie its very sophisticated design and mechanisation. A very real example of an energy-neutral house, it testifies to the fact that comfort and individuality need not be sacrificed for the sake of sustainability.

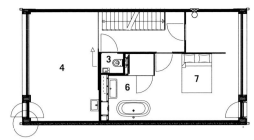

Third floor

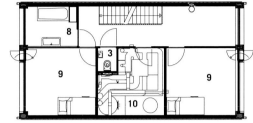

Second floor

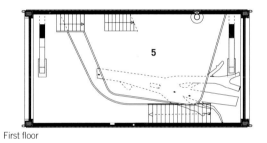

First floor

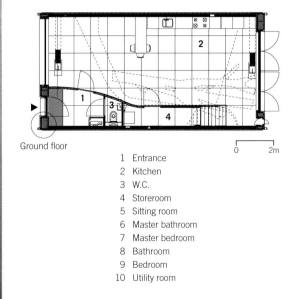

Ground floor

0   2m

1 Entrance
2 Kitchen
3 W.C.
4 Storeroom
5 Sitting room
6 Master bathroom
7 Master bedroom
8 Bathroom
9 Bedroom
10 Utility room

Tehama Grasshopper

San Francisco, California, USA

Fougeron Architecture

Photography: Matthew Millman, Richard Barnes

The east and west elevations are solid, structural walls with clerestory glazing, providing thermal mass and blocking excess heat from entering the building.

This remodelling of an under-utilised warehouse breaks down the rigidity of the original concrete structure in a subtle interplay of light, surfaces, levels, and indoor and outdoor spaces.

Perhaps the most stark transformation of this previously dark warehouse is the introduction of the abundance of natural light that pours in through the interior courtyard and the newly installed skylights. This not only reduces the need for artificial lighting but also opens the house up to dramatic vistas of the surrounding city skyline. High-efficiency dimmable T5 fluorescent tubes have been installed for when artificial lighting is required.

The penthouse floor is a completely new addition, with the large glazed windows on the north and south sides treated with a low-E coating, allowing natural light in but reducing solar gain and so moderating the internal temperature. The east and west elevations are solid, structural walls with clerestory glazing, providing thermal mass and blocking excess heat from entering the building.

The original warehouse's operable window system was kept, and the courtyard space has large sliding glass doors, allowing the natural circulation of air through the house. The sliding doors both on the main level and in the penthouse, combined with the open stairwell, produce a stack ventilation effect, passively cooling the house.

A radiant system in the concrete floors of the penthouse and the main level provides a form of heating more efficient than traditional forced-air systems and one that eliminates the need for ductwork. Other sustainable elements include low-VOC paint and other finishes in the interior, formaldehyde-free wall insulation, and a roof deck constructed of ipe wood, a highly durable and fast-growing timber species with FSC certification.

Overcoming constraints inherent in adapting a pre-existing structure, the multi-design-award-winning Tehama Grasshopper sees the transformation of a dark and dilapidated warehouse into a light and airy residential space that celebrates urban living and embraces the concept of sustainability.

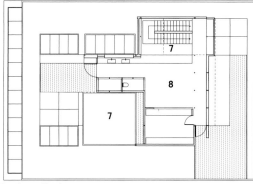

Penthouse/Roof

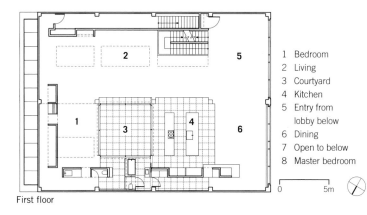

First floor

1 Bedroom
2 Living
3 Courtyard
4 Kitchen
5 Entry from
   lobby below
6 Dining
7 Open to below
8 Master bedroom

0   5m

Toten Farmhouse

Toten, Norway

Jarmund/Vigsnæs AS Architects MNAL

Photography: Nils Petter Dale

The barn's wooden cladding, more than 100 years old, was salvaged and used for the exterior cladding and terraces of the new house.

This house is located in the primarily agricultural district of Toten in the eastern part of Norway, near Lake Mjøsa, Norway's largest lake and one of Europe's deepest.

The sloping site originally consisted of an old farmhouse and barn. The barn had to be torn down because the main load-bearing structure was rotten, though the original farmhouse has been kept and is now used for storage and as a guesthouse. The barn's wooden cladding, more than 100 years old, was still in good condition, however, and was able to be salvaged and used for the exterior cladding and terraces of the new house. Many of these recycled planks have been cut to a width that varies from one end to the other, which is not only visually arresting but designed to adjust the horizontality of the cladding to the sloping ground and angle of the roof.

Efficient heating and insulation are important in this part of Norway, when during winter average maximum temperatures can hover around 0 °C (32 °F), dropping to around –8 °C (17.6 °F) at night. The main section of the house rises towards the south to allow warmth from the low winter sun to enter the building, while the glazed winter garden works as a heat collector during winter and a heat buffer for the rest of the house during summer. Heat is retained in the house as a result of the 40-centimetre-thick rock wool insulation in the roof structure and 20 centimetres in the walls. The exposed concrete ground floor provides thermal mass. The many windows on all sides of the house provide an abundance of natural light, and are aluminium-lined to prevent thermal bridging. The radiant floor heating system is backed up by a wood-burning stove when required.

The use of recycled timber in the construction of this house has not only maintained a historical context also but produced a low-embodied energy house that blends naturally with the remaining original farmhouse and surrounding woodland.

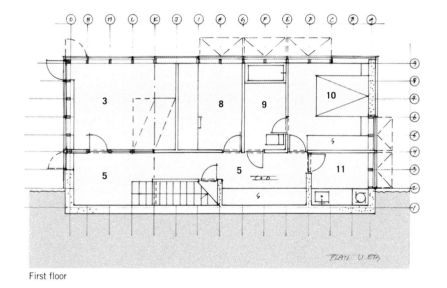

First floor

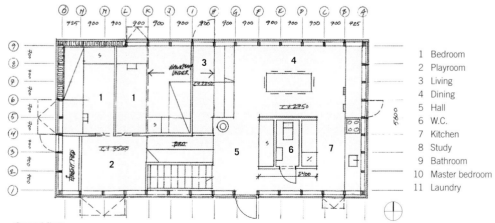

1 Bedroom
2 Playroom
3 Living
4 Dining
5 Hall
6 W.C.
7 Kitchen
8 Study
9 Bathroom
10 Master bedroom
11 Laundry

Ground floor

Treehouse

Hunter's Hill, NSW, Australia

Architecture Saville Isaacs

Photography: Kata Bayer, PRODUCT K

From the very beginning the intent was to create a house that sat lightly on the earth.

The Treehouse is a dual-occupancy residence located on a bushfront reserve in the Sydney suburb of Hunter's Hill. The total site area is 1600 square metres (17,222 square feet), with each dwelling roughly 180 square metres (1937 square feet) in size.

From the very beginning the intent was to create a house that sat lightly on the earth— a philosophy that was central to all aspects of the design. Careful consideration was given to the choice of materials used to ensure minimal impact on both the local and greater environment. Standard components were used in the construction to minimise embodied energy, floors and staircases were made of recycled timber, and only low-toxic laminates and finishes were applied.

The house is oriented to capture as much northern light as possible, allowing winter sunlight to penetrate deep into the living spaces while overhangs provide shade from the summer sun. Floors, walls, roof and ceilings are heavily insulated. The size and strategic positioning of openings creates natural cross-ventilation and assists with passive cooling. The elevation of the building off the site also takes advantage of natural breezes through the tree canopy.

Rainwater captured via the butterfly roof design is funnelled into the 10,000-litre rainwater tank located beneath each house. This water is then used for flushing toilets and watering the garden. There is also provision on the roof for the future installation of photovoltaic panels. Mains water is heated by means of an energy-efficient heat-exchange system.

The Treehouse demonstrates it is possible to create beautiful architecture using Ecologically Sustainable Design (ESD) principles and recycled, low-toxic and cost-effective materials. Through focusing on the interrelationship with the surrounding environment, volumetric quality and sculpted open spaces (enhanced by natural light), style is achieved without expensive finishes and aesthetic pretension.

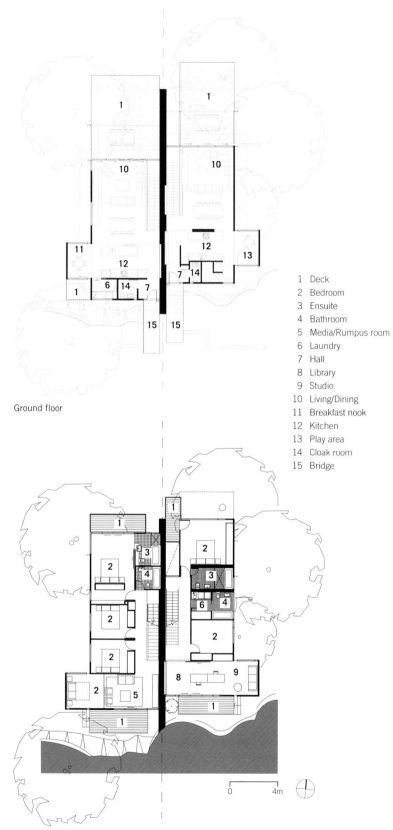

Ground floor

1 Deck
2 Bedroom
3 Ensuite
4 Bathroom
5 Media/Rumpus room
6 Laundry
7 Hall
8 Library
9 Studio
10 Living/Dining
11 Breakfast nook
12 Kitchen
13 Play area
14 Cloak room
15 Bridge

Lower ground floor

0   4m

Volga House

Alexino Village, Konakovsky District,
Tverskaya Region, Russia

Peter Kostelov

Photography: Alexey Knyazev

Operable windows allow for natural circulation, and cork panelling in certain sections of the roof and walls provides a sustainable form of insulation.

The 'green' credentials of wood (grows naturally, renewable, recyclable, stores carbon, low embodied energy) seem obvious, and yet these clear benefits are often overlooked when it comes to selecting building materials. This is not the case with the Volga house, however.

Located near the famous Volga River in Russia, this neat little three-storey house fits a lot into its relatively compact 133 square metres (1430 square feet). Built on a pre-existing stone block base, the house is constructed of various types of locally sourced wood treated and used in a range of interesting ways. The exterior patchwork-style woodwork, with its squares and rectangles of overlapping panels, hearkens back to the *dacha* (country house or villa) style houses of the Soviet era when, because of a scarcity

of materials, houses would be constructed of practically whatever could be found, with the result being dachas that reflected the patchwork nature of the various materials they were made of.

To create an interesting effect, the wooden panels have been painted various shades of brown and angled in such a way to reflect the sunlight in different ways. Some of the wood panelling consists of oriented strand board (OSB), a form of wood panelling made from layered strands of wood compressed and bonded together with wax and resin. When fast-growing, or sustainably forested, tree species are used it is an environmentally-friendly and efficient process that wastes very little timber and uses substantially less energy in its manufacture than many other building materials.

Strategically-placed windows allow a quite surprising amount of daylight to penetrate the house, lightening the tone and mood of the dark wood interior while dramatically brightening those parts of the house lined with lighter-coloured wood. Natural light also enters in interesting forms via the slits in the wood panelling. Operable windows allow for natural circulation, and cork panelling in certain sections of the roof and walls provides a sustainable form of insulation.

Dense and light, rustic and urban, traditional and modern, the Volga House is rich in contradictions and style without treading too heavily on the landscape.

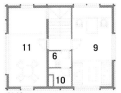
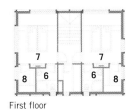

Second floor

First floor

Ground floor

1 Summer veranda
2 Living
3 Dining
4 Kitchen
5 Guest room
6 Bathroom
7 Bedroom
8 Wardrobe
9 Office
10 Sauna
11 Open terrace

Volga House

Glossary

Active solar design – harnessing and converting the sun's energy into usable power through mechanical or electrical equipment.

Bio-ethanol fireplace – fireplace that uses ethanol as a fuel source.

Blackwater – toilet waste water, or sewerage water.

Composite plastic/lumber – blend of recycled wood fibres and waste plastics commonly used for outdoor decking. Recyclable and doesn't contain the toxins found in treated wood.

Condensing boiler – system of heating that converts a greater percentage of fuel used into heat by 'condensing' and extracting heat from exhaust gases and water vapour.

Embodied energy – total amount of energy expended throughout the lifecycle of any material or product, including extraction of any raw materials, transportation, manufacturing and assembly, and end-of-life processes such as disassembly, recycling, destruction and decomposition.

Energy Recovery Ventilation (ERV) – energy efficient system of exchanging stale internal air with fresh outside air without impacting temperature. Also, heat recovery ventilation.

Forest Stewardship Council (FSC) certification – identifies a forest product as coming from a sustainably harvested and verifiable source.

Geothermal heating – form of heating that utilises the earth's natural store of heat.

Glazed windows – window panes are separated by a layer of air or gas to reduce heat transference. Double glazing (two window panes) is most common but triple glazing becoming increasingly popular.

Heat sink – a device that transfers heat generated within a solid object into, primarily, air or water.

Home Energy Rating System (HERS) index – system that rates the energy efficiency of a house against a HERS reference home (based on the 2006 International Energy Conservation Code). A rating lower than 100 means the house is more energy efficient than the reference home. For example, a score of 75 means a house is 25 per cent more efficient than the reference home.

Hydronic radiant floor heating – form of heating that utilises heat transfer from hot water circulating through a series of in-floor pipes. Water can be solar heated.

Insulated Concrete Form (ICF) – modular forms, or moulds, into which concrete is poured to form the walls, floors or roof of a house. The forms 'lock together' like building blocks, without the use of mortar, and can be made of polystyrene, polyurethane or cement-bonded wood fibre.

Leadership in Energy and Environmental Design (LEED) for Homes program – system developed by the US Green Building Council (USGBC) to rate the sustainability of residential homes. The LEED rating system covers eight broad areas, including energy and atmosphere, water efficiency, materials and resources, and indoor environmental quality. Depending on a house's LEED score (out of a possible 100, with some extra points awarded in certain categories), the following certification levels are possible—Certified, Silver, Gold and Platinum.

Low Emissivity (low-E) glass – glass with a special coating designed to reflect radiant heat.

Masonry heater/stove – primarily wood-burning heater with a relatively large surface area that radiates heat for long periods of time.

Oriented Strand Boards (OSB) – form of wood panelling made from layered strands of wood compressed and bonded together with wax and resin.

Passive solar design – use of solar energy through non-mechanical and non-electrical means. Windows oriented to maximise solar gain is an example of passive solar design.

Phase Changing Materials (PCMs) – a substance capable of storing and releasing a large amount of energy. PCMs store energy by changing phase from solid to liquid (melting) and releasing heat by changing phase from liquid to solid (freezing).

Rigid insulation – construction material (generally polystyrene or polyurethane) that gives thermal resistance to walls, foundations and roofs. The thermal resistance of rigid insulation is measured by the material's R-value. The higher the R-value, the more resistant it is to temperature transfer.

Structural Insulated Panel (SIP) – panel consisting of rigid polymer foam sandwiched between two structural boards, most commonly OSB.

Solar gain, or heat gain – rise in temperature resulting from solar radiation.

Solar chimney, also thermal chimney, stack ventilation – system of natural circulation in which the air heated within the 'chimney' rises, pulling in cooler air at the chimney's base, ventilating and passively cooling the surrounding area.

Solar reflectance – the level at which a material or surface reflects solar radiation.

Thermal bridge – pathway through which heat escapes/flows, created by the joining of materials with poor thermal insulation properties.

Thermal mass – a material's capacity to absorb, store and radiate heat. A material with high thermal mass helps to stabilise temperature by absorbing heat when the surrounding temperature rises, and letting that heat out when the surrounding temperature cools.

Thermal resistance – the degree to which a material resists the transfer of heat.

Volatile Organic Compounds (VOCs) – often toxic chemicals used in certain paints, polishes and finishes that can have harmful health effects.

Index of Architects